CW00971585

BRIGHT N____

TRISTRAM SHANDY BY LAURENCE STERNE

Intelligent Education

INFLUENCE PUBLISHERS

Nashville, Tennessee

BRIGHT NOTES: Tristram Shandy

www.BrightNotes.com

No part of this publication may be used or reproduced in any manner whatsoever without written permission, except in the case of brief quotations in critical articles and reviews. For permissions, contact Influence Publishers http://www.influencepublishers.com.

ISBN: 978-1-645424-08-6 (Paperback)

ISBN: 978-1-645424-09-3 (eBook)

Published in accordance with the U.S. Copyright Office Orphan Works and Mass Digitization report of the register of copyrights, June 2015.

Originally published by Monarch Press.

David A. Gooding, 1966

2019 Edition published by Influence Publishers.

Interior design by Lapiz Digital Services. Cover Design by Thinkpen Designs.

Printed in the United States of America.

Library of Congress Cataloging-in-Publication Data forthcoming.

Names: Intelligent Education

Title: BRIGHT NOTES: Tristram Shandy

Subject: STU004000 STUDY AIDS / Book Notes

CONTENTS

INTRODUCTION TO LAURENCE STERNE

LAURENCE STERNE IN HIS TIME

Among eighteenth-century novelists, Laurence Sterne stands out as one of the most engaging, and at the same time one of the most puzzling, figures. If we were to form an estimate of him based upon the remarks of his contemporaries, we would find, not a single portrait, but a bewildering variety of them. To some of his friends Sterne was the hard-working and ambitious parish clergyman and small landowner, to others the companion of riotous nights spent in drinking and telling tall tales, to still others the brilliant and incisive political pamphleteer. A surprisingly large circle of elegant women thought of him as the soulful, sentimental and occasionally passionate suitor, while his London friends, looking at him in the light of his great work, *Tristram Shandy*, perceived the witty and eccentric clergyman and accomplished socialite, equally ready to make the drawing room weep with a romantic tale or set it roaring with a bawdy one. All of these pictures of Sterne are true ones; he was a man with an extraordinary diversity both of talents and of masks which he presented to the outside world. Part of the confusion which surrounds Sterne has its origin in the contrast between the (relative) conventionality of his life and the wild unconventionality of his work. To understand this fascinating man we must first look at the age that produced him, which was itself an age of contradictions.

BACKGROUND: ENGLAND IN THE EIGHTEENTH CENTURY

England, during Sterne's life (he lived from 1713 to 1768) was prosperous, class-conscious, beginning to realize its influence as an international power. The English had a strongly developed sense of national identity and pride, but there were threats to stability as a result of religious divisions between Presbyterians (Dissenters), Catholics, and members of the Church of England (the Established Church), and because of the political rivalry between Whigs and Tories. The Established Church, with its Episcopalian religious tenets, was supported by the government; its clergymen formed a solidly entrenched class, fiercely jealous of its rights and privileges. The decision to enter the Church was rarely a call to the religious life, but far more often simply a method of making a living without excessive effort, and often a very prosperous one. Appointments to a parish church (significantly, they were called "livings") were often controlled by local magnates or the nobility. A clergyman with influence could frequently get himself appointed rector of a number of parishes, thus collecting the fixed income connected with each church while appointing a subordinate at a nominal wage to do the actual parish work. This custom was called "pluralism," and although religious reformers objected to it, it was an accepted and very widespread practice.

THE CLIMATE OF LITERATURE

The eighteenth century's golden age of literature, the Augustan Age (roughly the first quarter of the century) was over by the time Sterne was old enough to take an interest in such things. In matters of taste, however, Augustan cleverness and elegance, together with that elusive quality called wit, were still highly prized. At the same time the literate public was rapidly expanding, and the lower-class portion of it was demanding more excitement, scandal and sentiment in its reading matter. With the publication of Samuel Richardson's Pamela in 1740, the novel became an accepted form. As we shall see, Sterne in his own writing tried to cater to all sectors of the reading public, and he was sufficiently in tune with his era to produce almost exactly what it wanted to read. In *Tristram Shandy* he combined wit and sentiment in a format which is part novel, part essay, partly indescribable and wholly original.

STERNE'S EARLY YEARS

Laurence Sterne was born in the small Irish town of Clonmel on November 24, 1713. His ancestors had been people of some importance in England; a great-grandfather was Archbishop of York, but Laurence's father was an impoverished career officer in the Army who never rose above the rank of lieutenant. The author's boyhood seems to have been relatively uneventful, except for the fact that he fell into a mill stream and was swept under the turning mill wheel, to emerge bruised but alive on the other side. His extraordinary survival made him, temporarily, a local celebrity. Financial help from relatives enabled him to go to school in England, and despite the death of his father when Laurence was eighteen, he entered Jesus College, Cambridge, in 1733. A number of the young man's relatives were clergymen, and the Church seemed the obvious and in fact the only sensible professional career for him. Sterne received a B.A. from Cambridge in 1737 and the M.A. in 1740. During his college years he revealed the first symptoms of the tuberculosis which would periodically make him an invalid in later life and eventually cause his death.

THE RISING YOUNG CLERGYMAN

At this crucial point in his career Sterne came under the wing of his uncle, Dr. Jaques Sterne, Precentor of York. (The Precentorship was an important ecclesiastical office connected with York Cathedral.) Dr. Sterne was a fanatical Whig, one of the many Church of England clergymen who supported the policies of the crafty Whig Prime Minister, Sir Robert Walpole, and opposed the return to the throne of the Stuart line in the person of Bonnie Prince Charles. It seems clear that Dr. Sterne intended to use his nephew's literary talents to fight his own political battles. With the help of his uncle's influence, Laurence was ordained to the priesthood and made vicar of the parish of Sutton-in-the-Forest, just north of the city of York, in 1738, with an annual income of forty pounds. In 1741, after a courtship marked by effusive letters which read like excerpts from Sterne's *Sentimental Journey*, he married Elizabeth Lumley. Sterne's was a typical eighteenth-century marriage. When his friends commented on the "suitability" of the union, they meant that the income from Elizabeth's small fortune matched the young vicar's own salary. For a number of years the future author busied himself with writing political pamphlets for this uncle, managing parish affairs and farming the lands attached to his parsonage, varying these activities by occasional visits to his college friend John Hall-Stevenson. The companions who assembled at the house of this wealthy and lively young squire, for sessions of roistering, drinking, and storytelling, called themselves the "Demoniacks." They christened Hall-Stevenson's estate "Crazy Castle," but their activities seem to have been more high-spirited than vicious. Few people expressed any surprise that Sterne, a clergyman, should take part in such goings-on. Two events now conspired to turn Sterne's thoughts toward writing for publication and profit. The first was the success of his satire on a conniving attorney, called *The History of a Good Warm Watchcoat*. The work is indebted to the English satirist Jonathan Swift, especially to Swift's **burlesque** on religious rivalry entitled *The Tale of a Tub*. The other event was Laurence's quarrel with his uncle, Dr. Jaques Sterne, which blocked any chance for the nephew's further advancement in the Church.

THE LITERARY LION

At the age of forty-six, Sterne turned his thoughts to a full-length comic or satirical work for the London literary market. In 1760 the first two volumes of *Tristram Shandy* appeared, their publication subsidized in part by the author himself. In spite of initial difficulties in finding a London publisher, the book instantly caught the fancy of the public and Sterne arrived at the capital to find himself the toast of the season. Celebrities and noblemen vied for the privilege of his presence at their social functions, and the somewhat uncouth country parson blossomed out with amazing rapidity into a well-dressed, confident man-about-town. A story from this period demonstrates that advertising is not an invention of the twentieth century. Early in 1760 David Garrick, the famous Shakespearean actor, received a letter from an acquaintance named Catherine Fourmantelle, a French singer who was then at York, telling him of a two-volume comic novel named *Tristram Shandy*, "which have made a great noise and have had a prodigious run." When Garrick told his friends, who included all the literary lights of London, about this fascinating new book, he had no suspicion that Miss Fourmantelle had written her letter at the dictation of - the Reverend Laurence Sterne.

TRAVELS ABROAD

From the first part of *Tristram Shandy* and a volume of sermons which he rushed into print to "follow up" his success, Sterne realized the large sum of 830 pounds. He was able to buy a fine coach and horses with which to return to York. But although the author's finances were better, his health was worse. He worked furiously on a continuation of his popular fantasy and published Books III and IV in January, 1761, and the fifth and sixth volumes in November of the same year. Now his health was really failing under the combined effects of overwork and tuberculosis, and the doctors strongly recommended travel abroad. January of 1762 found the literary parson in Paris, where his conquest of London was repeated, and he made firm friends with the French author Denis Diderot. After being joined by his wife, and his daughter, Lydia, he went south to the warmer climate of Toulouse. Sterne was not a man to waste good material, and a comic description of travel in France became the subject of one of the succeeding sections of *Tristram Shandy*. The Sternes remained in France for over two years. When the time to return arrived a long series of quarrels between Sterne and his wife came to a head with Elizabeth's declaration that she was going to stay on the Continent. The author's only recorded objection to this arrangement was a financial one. Apparently Sterne felt that his numerous London flirtations, harmless as they may have been, could be carried out more comfortably if Mrs. Sterne was in France. January, 1765, saw the publication of the seventh and eighth volumes of *Tristram Shandy*, and two more volumes of sermons appeared in the same year. By October Sterne was in Italy, and this trip, as well as parts of the previous one, form the geographical basis for *A Sentimental Journey Through France and Italy*. The last volume of *Tristram Shandy* appeared in 1767, and the Sentimental Journey in 1768. The emotional background for the Sentimental Journey is provided by the last and perhaps the only truly passionate affair of Sternes life, his courtship (though his wife was still alive) of Elizabeth Draper, the wife of a government official stationed in India. The affair is also recorded in his private Journal to Eliza, maintained for a number of months in 1767 after Elizabeth's return to her husband in the East. Sterne's last amour and the books which resulted from it have been seen as the feverish activity of a dying man. The author's health was failing fast; in March he caught the influenza that was raging in London and quickly succumbed. A last macabre note might have amused the writer who included so many jibes at death in his works. Sterne's corpse was dug up by the body-snatchers (or "resurrection men") and sold as a specimen for dissection to an Oxford surgeon. According to the story, one of Sterne's friends recognized the body on the dissecting-table and fainted.

TRISTRAM SHANDY

Without some warning about the Shandean "system," or rather lack of system, *Tristram Shandy* can at first be rather baffling. Anyone who reads it expecting to find some similarity to other eighteenth-century novels will be disappointed. For Sterne's work is almost wholly unconventional, an experiment in a new kind of writing, though aspects of Sterne's style find their roots in earlier literature. In particular, the author admires and acknowledges his debt to the fantastic episodes, the incredible catalogs and bawdy asides of the French master humorist of the sixteenth century, Francois Rabelais, the author of *Gargantua and Pantagruel*. Hardly less important is the picturesque humor and romantic digressions of the Spanish writer Miguel de Cervantes' *Don Quixote*. And to complete the acknowledged debts, Sterne bows to the discursive and highly personal essays of the French author Michel de Montaigne and his English counterpart Robert Burton, the creator of the *Anatomy of Melancholy*. All of these writers experimented with new literary forms, and Sterne takes license from their freedom. He writes a book which deals not with actions but with opinions, which derives relationships not from humdrum laws of cause and effect but from the English philosopher John Locke's theory of the association of ideas. In *Tristram Shandy* time does not depend on the clock but is wholly subjective.

ORGANIZATION OF TRISTRAM SHANDY

In spite of this seeming confusion, there is a good deal of order in *Tristram Shandy*. An overall pattern is present: the action of the first two volumes takes place immediately before the birth of Tristram, and much of the argument, speculation and reflection is based upon his imminent arrival. We meet the principal characters: Tristram's father, Walter; his military Uncle Toby, and Toby's servant, Corporal Trim; the obstetrician or accoucheur, as he prefers to be called, Dr. Slop; and Parson Yorick, who in some aspects is Sterne himself. Books III and IV begin the tale of Tristram's misfortunes, the accident to his nose, and the erroneous christening, and also include the long digression of the German philosopher Slawkenbergius. In the fifth and sixth books Tristram meets with another accident and we are given the sentimental story of Le Fever. In Books VII and VIII Sterne turns to his travels on the Continent for material, and begins the long-promised tale of Uncle Toby's courtship of the Widow Wadman. The final volume provides the end of the affair between the innocent Uncle Toby and the Widow Wadman, but at this point death wrote finis to a work which Sterne might have carried on forever.

THE PURPOSE OF TRISTRAM SHANDY

Sterne's first intention is to make us laugh, and we feel that if he can do that he is quite satisfied. He has no objection, however, if we think as well, and there is food for thought in much of his humor. He makes us consider the limitations of the logic in which we put such trust, the value of theories which remain purely theoretical, and the absurdity of our ideas of time in a world where everything is relative. Some of the greatest books of modern times, James oyce's *Ulysses*, Marcel Proust's *Remembrance of Things Past*, and Thomas ann's *The Magic Mountain*, among others, have questioned the same far-reaching assumptions that Sterne is skeptical of, but few of them have one it with his good humor, or with his saving sense of the ridiculous.

TRISTRAM SHANDY

BOOK I

CHAPTERS 1–5

The narrator of the tale is Tristram Shandy himself, but the story as he tells it begins well before his birth. Tristram complains that his father and mother were momentarily distracted at the instant of his conception, and that many of the misfortunes of his life can be traced to this inattention.

Comment: Tristram tells the story, but we can assume that the author uses him to voice his own ideas a good deal of the time. While the physical description of the hero of the book does not fit Laurence Sterne very well, the personality and especially the ideas of the narrator match those of Sterne perfectly. Readers who find the apparently disjointed and wandering style of *Tristram Shandy* confusing should refer to the discussions of the "Shandean style" in the Introduction and Critical Commentary. From the

beginning the author takes a very intimate tone with the reader, addressing him directly in asides and explaining things to him. In this way Sterne tries to ingratiate himself with his audience, to make them become involved in the action of the story and at the same time to amuse them with his odd approach to writing. Later on he deliberately tricks his readers a number of times; he can only do this if he is on good terms with them.

The narrator gives an elaborate explanation of how the child's whole future may hang in the balance at the moment when he first comes into being. At the crucial time, his mother asks his father if he has wound the clock, and, for Tristram, the damage is done. The "animal spirits" which under proper conditions should inspire the newly conceived child will always be lacking.

Comment: In his remarks about the "Homunculus" ("little man") Sterne is referring to the belief current during this period that the fertilized egg is a tiny human being, perfect in every detail.

Tristram's father, Walter, and his uncle Toby, two of the main characters in the book, are introduced in Chapter 3. His father is a philosopher and delights in speculating at length about the most obscure points. His son, who seems to enjoy explaining things at equal length, points out that readers are insatiably curious about the characters of a story. For once, their curiosity will be satisfied. They will find out all about the hero's life; the tale will begin ab ovo (literally, "from the egg"). Tristram is begotten on a Sunday night early in March of 1718. His father makes it an invariable habit to wind the clock on Sunday night and because of this custom, his mother is prompted to ask the fatal question.

Comment: The author pauses here to comment on the English philosopher John Locke's theory of the association of ideas. Sterne was fascinated by Locke's work, particularly the famous Essay Concerning Human Understanding, and in *Tristram Shandy* he returns again and again to his theories, playing with them and using them for humorous effects. Some critics maintain that the philosophical basis of Sterne's book is an attempt to show the limitations of Locke's completely rational approach to life. Communication takes place and things get done, says Sterne, even when people behave in the most irrational way.

CHAPTERS 6–10

In the midst of a spate of asides to the reader, we learn the history of the local midwife, whose instruction and license have been paid for by the parson, Yorick.

Comment: Yorick, who does not appear in person as yet, is a second alter ego for Sterne, this time in his position as clergyman.

The eighth and ninth chapters are devoted to a mock, all-purpose introduction, which the author offers to any member of the nobility who may want it at the price of fifty guineas.

Comment: It was customary at this time to dedicate books to famous people, particularly rich members of the nobility. The unspoken understanding was that the person so addressed would show his gratitude for the honor in hard cash. Sterne is, of course, making fun of the custom.

In Chapter 10 we learn more of the history of Parson Yorick. He cuts a figure of fun on a broken-down horse that looks like Rosinante, the steed of Don Quixote in Cervantes' novel. Luckily, Yorick himself can see the humor of the situation.

> **Comment: Cervantes'** ***Don Quixote*,** **the famous Spanish comic novel of the sixteenth century, is another major source of inspiration for Sterne. He was particularly impressed by the sentimental and pathetic interludes in the work, and many of the sentimental scenes of** ***Tristram Shandy*** **are modeled upon them, at least in spirit.**

CHAPTERS 11–15

The name Yorick is the same as that of the jester in Shakespeare's *Hamlet*; Prince Hamlet, musing over the dead clown's skull, begins the famous speech, "Alas, poor Yorick." Perhaps, Tristram speculates, Parson Yorick is a lineal descendant of the Danish jester. At least he has inherited the wit, for like his ancestor he can often "set the table in a roar." Tristram says that he has had no time to check on this business of ancestry in his travels through Europe, because he was acting as tutor to a young gentleman. He promises to give an account of their travels later in the book. All he had a chance to see was that the Danes were sensible, rather stolid people, and this fact argues against Yorick's Danish ancestry, for the parson is merry and whimsical to a fault.

> **Comment: In his private letters and even in his published sermons Sterne used the pen name of Yorick. As the author of** ***Tristram Shandy*** **he deliberately created a public image of himself as the humorous, even scatterbrained clergyman, identical with the Parson Yorick of the book.**

Yorick is warned by his friend Eugenius that people who wish him ill will take advantage of his open and careless disposition. In fact, things turn out just as Eugenius predicts; Yorick, though completely innocent, is the victim of a conspiracy which thwarts all his hopes of becoming a bishop someday.

> **Comment: Yorick's friend Eugenius was in real life Sterne's friend John Hall-Stevenson, at whose house, "Crazy Castle," the "Demoniacks" met for entertainment. The portrait of Eugenius as the wise and sober friend must be either ironic or intentionally flattering - Hall-Stevenson was neither. The "plot" which Yorick complains of was a real one, the result of his quarrel with his influential uncle, Dr. Jaques Sterne. Dr. Sterne not only used his influence with the authorities of York Cathedral to block further promotion for his nephew, but spread the rumor that Laurence had neglected his mother so shamefully that she was forced to enter the poorhouse.**

An account of Yorick's last hours is now given' together with a description of his grave and **epitaph**, "Alas, poor Yorick!" Sterne closes the sentimental account with a Shandean trick on the reader, a large black rectangle printed at the end of Yorick's history as a memorial and symbol of mourning.

The story now veers back to the midwife, but only momentarily. Tristram's attention is distracted by the question of why he was born where he was, and this problem can only be solved by reference to his mother's marriage settlement. The settlement is produced verbatim in Chapter 15, in a long **parody** of legal phraseology. We finally discover that Mrs. Shandy is allowed by the terms of the settlement to return to her parents' home in London during her pregnancy. However, if it should happen that she is not really pregnant, then she forfeits the right to go to London the next time. This is just what has happened in Tristram's case; the year previously there had been a "false alarm," and thus our hero is doomed to all the dangers of being born in the country.

CHAPTERS 16-20

Tristram's mother, forced by his father's obstinancy to have her child away from London, picks out the midwife whom we have already met to deliver her, refusing the services of a doctor who specializes in obstetrics. His father, a little ashamed of being so stubborn, and concerned for his wife's safety, arranges that the doctor will wait downstairs during the delivery in case of emergency. There follows a digression on the importance of Christian names. Mr. Shandy is convinced that the name a child is given affects his whole future life; a "good" name, such as Caesar, or even William, can be very helpful, but there can be no hope for someone with a "bad" name, such as Tristram. In fact, Tristram is the worst possible name.

At this point Sterne changes direction once more to accuse his readers, especially the female ones, of reading without proper attention because they fail to realize that Mrs. Shandy is not a Roman Catholic. There was an obvious hint in the statement that Tristram had to be born before he could be baptized. He then proceeds to make fun of the Roman Catholic belief (according to Sterne) that children can be baptized before they are born, if some part of the body can be seen. He presses this question to its logical, but absurd, conclusion; why cannot the infant be baptized in the womb by means of a syringe? A learned dissertation on the question, in French, and supposedly by the Doctors of the Sorbonne, is included here. In the end they come to no conclusion at all, but refer the matter to the local bishop and the Pope.

> **Comment: As a result of passages like this one, Sterne has been accused of writing in bad taste, and with perfect justice. His emphasis on the physical seemed especially deplorable to Victorian readers, who branded him obscene. The reader should realize, however, that rather coarse jokes on bodily functions and the physical side of life were accepted fare in Sterne's time, and his book shocked very few of his contemporaries. At the same time, the Roman Catholics were fair game for any sort of abuse, especially for a patriotic Anglican clergyman such as Sterne. The Catholic minority in England was considered a threat to national unity and a potentially subversive element. During Sterne's tenure at Sutton-in-the Forest, in 1745, Scotland rose for Charles Stuart, grandson of James II, and with Catholic backing his army managed to push well south into England before his defeat at Culloden.**

CHAPTERS 21–25

The reader is returned to the scene of Tristram's imminent birth, but only long enough to give Sterne the occasion for dashing away in a new direction. This time the subject is Uncle Toby, and especially the peculiarities of his character. The unusual variations in the English climate, the author speculates, are what give rise to the extraordinary eccentricity of the English temperament. Having advanced this new theory, he applauds himself for having added to the sum of scientific knowledge.

All the male Shandys are "originals," (that is, their characters are highly eccentric) while the females "had no character at all." What distinguishes Uncle Toby is an extraordinary modesty, the result of being hit in the groin by a piece of stone dislodged by a cannonball at the siege of Namur.

The only exception to the uniform mildness of the Shandy women is Great Aunt Dinah, who distinguished herself by marrying the coachman. Uncle Toby feels that this skeleton in the family cupboard should be decently concealed, but Tristram's father is forever bringing it to light as a subject for "philosophical" speculation. Toby's innate good temper does not allow him to protest too vehemently at this; he contents himself with whistling "Lillabullero."

Comment: "Lillabullero" is a satirical Irish ballad which pokes fun at the government in a thinly disguised fashion. For Uncle Toby, whistling the song is a means of relieving his feelings as well as implying that what he is forced to listen to is a pack of nonsense. It is his favorite recourse when he is brought to a conversational impasse.

Tristram now points out that the action of the story progresses even during his digression, a unique advantage of his kind of writing. He also hints that by this method he can make the book go on for volume after volume, just as long as he wishes. Chapter 23, he proposes, should start "very nonsensically," and he introduces a discussion of Momus's glass, a device for seeing into men's souls. Since Momus's glass does not actually exist, the process of drawing literary characters without this mechanical aid is very difficult. As a result, he has decided to draw Uncle

Toby's character in a new way, by means of his hobby-horse. He carefully avoids telling the reader what this hobby-horse is until the next book.

> **Comment: The subject of hobby-horses, to which Sterne returns again and again, seems to have caught his fancy particularly. He means by the term the kind of hobby or consuming interest to which some people devote all their energies, and which unconsciously rules the whole course of their lives. Sterne found this disposition to be totally absorbed in something which is essentially trivial one of the most intriguing absurdities of the human personality.**

TRISTRAM SHANDY

BOOK II

....

CHAPTERS 1–5

The siege of Namur, as the occasion of Uncle Toby's wound, occupies a central place in his mind, and he is tormented by the fact that the engagement is almost too complicated to explain to his listeners. At length, all his interest is focused upon it, and it becomes his hobby-horse. The author breaks off here to show his readers why even someone as intelligent as Toby should have difficulty explaining things, and refers them to Locke's *Essay Concerning Human Understanding*. "The problem has three roots: dull perception, transient impressions made by the things seen, and a poor memory".

Uncle Toby now purchases a map of the battlefield so that he can show his friends exactly where his wound was received. He falls in love with the map, and goes on to maps of other battlefields and fortified towns, and to works on military history and theory. He moves on from this study to ballistics, geometry and trigonometry, and all the other sciences connected with warfare.

> **Comment: Walter Shandy and Uncle Toby are related by blood, but also in their mentality. While his brother pursues his philosophical speculations to their often absurd conclusions, Toby, displaying another aspect of the same temperament, goes riding off, unchecked, on his hobbyhorse.**

All this indoor study of battlefields makes Toby long to have his wound cured so that he can get out into the open air again. His servant, Corporal Trim, suggests making a large scale model of the fortifications out of doors, under Uncle Toby's direction; here they can re-enact the whole Flanders campaign if they wish to. The old soldier's imagination is instantly fired by this project, and he can hardly wait to get to his brother's country estate to begin it.

CHAPTERS 6–10

We are suddenly returned by the author to Shandy Hall, where Mrs. Shandy's labor pains are coming on. The maid runs for the midwife, while Mr. Shandy sends for Dr. Slop, the man-midwife (obstetrician).

> **Comment: The "Dr. Slop" of *Tristram Shandy* was a real person, Dr. John Burton of York, one of the pioneers in the science of obstetrics. In his politics he was an extreme Tory, which made Sterne his political enemy, and the vicar never missed a chance to pillory him, in his book or in pamphlets.**

Uncle Toby suggests that Mrs. Shandy refuses to see Dr. Slop because she is too modest to let a man come near her at such a delicate time. His brother, nervous and irritable during this critical time, declares that the remark is a stupid one; Toby is so naive that he does not even know which is the right end of a woman. Upon reflection, Toby admits that this is true. Relapsing into philosophy, Mr. Shandy is just about to explain the difference between the right and wrong ends of a woman when there is a thunderous knock at the door.

Sterne now launches into a complicated discussion of the nature of time. His starting point is: Has there been enough time for the servant to fetch Dr. Slop, while the reader has been occupied with the intervening pages? He reminds us that the idea of duration (that is, of the passage of time) is derived from the succession of ideas. When we think of one idea, and then of a second one, we know that time has passed.

Comment: The digression on time provides a typical example of the way Sterne takes serious philosophical or scientific ideas as a basis for humorous speculation. The theory that the duration of time proceeds from the succession of ideas is borrowed wholly from the philosopher John Locke. Locke is trying to analyze in a scientific way just what time is. Sterne, on the other hand, shows us that despite all such analysis, time is essentially subjective. Just how much time has really elapsed since the servant was sent for Dr. Slop? The author responds by asking, "Whose time?" The servant's time, plowing through the muddy roads; Walter Shandy's time, immersed in philosophical speculation; Tristram's mother's time, enduring the pangs of childbirth; the author's time, during which he has told us all about Toby's military campaign, his

wound, and a four-year convalescence; none of these
intervals is equal to another, yet each is equally "real."

Once the reader has become thoroughly immersed in this theory,
Sterne turns the tables once again by telling us that the servant
did not have to ride sixteen miles for Dr. Slop after all, but met
him sixty yards from the house. Dr. Slop encounters Obadiah,
the servant, in full career on a great coach-horse and is tumbled
headlong among the puddles. As he is ushered into the house,
dripping mud, Dr. Slop amply lives up to his name.

CHAPTERS 11–15

To make matters worse, Dr. Slop has only come to visit the
Shandys on the off-chance that he might be needed, and has
left all his obstetrical instruments behind. Obadiah sets out
once more to get them. In the interim, the doctor and the
Shandy brothers sit down at the fire, and Uncle Toby relates the
succession of ideas which the sudden appearance of Dr. Slop
has brought to his mind. The connection he makes is, of course,
concerned with fortifications and particularly with the engineer
Stevinus; he goes off into a long dissertation on the subject until
his brother impatiently interrupts.

**Comment: Here Sterne is again having fun with
Locke's theories about the association of ideas.**

Corporal Trim is sent for Stevinus' book and is told to look for
a picture of Stevinus' famous sailing chariot. He cannot find the
picture, but shakes the book and out falls a sermon.

CHAPTERS 16–19

Trim is asked if he is able to read the sermon, and declares proudly that he can because he has served as clerk to the chaplain of the regiment. He proceeds to read the address which has as its text a sentence from St. Paul's Epistle to the Hebrews, "For we trust that we have a good conscience." The writer of the document sets out to refute the implications of this statement; he maintains that we sometimes persuade ourselves not to feel guilty when actually we should. The reading is frequently interrupted by the remarks of Dr. Slop, who is a Catholic, and of the Shandy brothers.

> **Comment: The sermon (called "The Abuses of Conscience") is a real one which Laurence Sterne wrote and delivered at York Cathedral. It was one of his favorite techniques (related to his method in *Tristram Shandy*) to explain his text by pretending to disprove it. This approach both shocked and intrigued his audience. In writing his novel Sterne was not too fussy about the originality of his material. He made use of his own earlier writing, including pamphlets, private letters, and sermons such as this one, and on occasion also borrowed heavily from his favorite authors.**

Every mention in the sermon, which is a long one, of battles or fortifications immediately sets Uncle Toby off on a military digression, while Corporal Trim, who has a soft heart, is deeply affected by the trials of the imaginary people in the text. The Shandys decide that the sermon, by its style and manner, must be one of Parson Yorick's.

Obadiah now comes in with Dr. Slop's obstetrical instruments, and all present are reminded of what is going on upstairs. Walter

Shandy, a little embarrassed, explains to the doctor that he has agreed with his wife not to let Slop attend her unless there is an emergency. The author now pauses to explain a little more of Mr. Shandy's character. He always insists on taking the opposite point of view to everyone else, and quibbling over tiny points because, he says, it is uncertainty on these small matters which can bring the whole structure of a philosophical argument down in ruins.

Walter has a very definite reason for wanting Dr. Slop to attend his wife. He feels that a man's wits, and thus his success in life, must proceed from his soul. But the souls of all men are essentially the same - then why do some men succeed so much better than others? It must be because the place in their bodies that contains the soul is disturbed in some cases and Tristram's father sets out to find where this place is. It has to be somewhere in the head, he theorizes, because all the nerves are centered there. In that case, the pressure to which the head is subjected during the process of birth will, under normal conditions, seriously disturb the soul. Walter Shandy wishes to guard against this accident to his son. It would be much safer, he concludes, to have the child extracted feet first, for the chance that most deliveries are head foremost accounts for the fact that most people are such fools. As for what resulted from this theory, Sterne tells us, the reader must be content to wait until next year, for here the book ends for the time being.

Comment: As the Introduction points out, *Tristram Shandy* was published at the rate of two volumes a year, and the end of the first published volume occurs here. It was in Sterne's interest to make it a "cliff-hanging" ending, and he does so, although the structure of the book is so disorganized that stopping at any other place would have served to keep the audience in suspense almost as well.

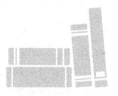

TRISTRAM SHANDY

TEXTUAL ANALYSIS

BOOK III

. . . .

CHAPTERS 1–10

A remark directed by Uncle Toby to Dr. Slop, "I wish you had seen what prodigious armies we had in Flanders," rather staggers the medical man because it seems to have no connection with what has gone before. Walter attempts to relieve the awkward atmosphere by answering his brother, but in doing so he takes off his wig to mop his brow, and makes a ridiculous figure of himself by straining to get his left hand into his right hand pocket. The mischance angers Walter, and provides Sterne with the occasion for a short digression on anger and on Uncle Toby's mildness.

Obadiah having now come in with the doctor's instruments (as he already had some six chapters back), Dr. Slop finds that he has tied up the mouth of the bag with a series of impossible knots and expends much bad language trying to untie them. It is more difficult to deliver the instruments out of the bag than to deal with Mrs. Shandy herself. The obstetrical expert decides to cut the cord, and in doing so slashes his thumb to the bone.

At this Walter Shandy cannot resist pointing out what loss of temper and excessive cursing over a small matter may lead to. He has recently come across, he says, a most interesting and explicit form of swearing in a manuscript, and he gives Dr. Slop the document to read aloud. In doing this he is playing a joke on the Roman Catholic physician, for the text he gives him is the formal sentence of excommunication as pronounced by Ernulf, the Catholic Bishop of Rochester in medieval times, which is recorded in the Textus Roffensis.

CHAPTERS 11–19

Chapter 11 is devoted to the full Latin text of the anathema, with a parallel English translation, including the insertion of the name of Obadiah in the proper places; there are pauses which enable Uncle Toby to make comments or whistle "Lillabullero." The doctor soon discovers that he is reading a Catholic document that was meant to be taken seriously, but feels that there is no hope for it now, and plows on to the end.

> **Comment: The document given here is apparently a genuine medieval Latin sentence of excommunication, or banishment from the Roman Catholic Church as punishment for some serious crime. Sterne and most of his Anglican contemporaries would have been surprised to learn that future generations would consider mockery of someone else's religion in bad taste. As far as they were concerned, those outside the Episcopal Church, and particularly the Catholics, were fair game.**

As a conclusion to the digression on swearing, Sterne comments that we only flatter ourselves when we think we have invented original oaths; they are all to be found, worked out and more elaborately and poetically too, in Bishop Ernulf's document. Tristram's father considers this anathema a kind of text or reference work on the art of bad language.

Though all this time has gone by, Mrs. Shandy's labor has not progressed. The midwife asks Dr. Slop to come upstairs to consult with her, but the doctor suggests that proper subordination be observed - she should come down to talk to him. In the meantime he proudly pulls out of his bag a pair of forceps, which he has designed himself. Their proper use is demonstrated on Uncle Toby, who clenches his two fists to the size of a baby's head, but the doctor succeeds only in taking all the skin off Toby's knuckles. Dr. Slop adds that it is very important to determine if the child is presenting the head or the hip, "because, Sir, if the hip is mistaken for the head-there is a possibility (if it is a boy) that the forceps **********."

> **Comment: The doctor refers here, of course, to the danger of castrating the infant. While it would be unwise to apply psychological analysis to so whimsical a work as *Tristram Shandy*, there is no doubt that the theme of castration and the fear of it run all through the book, from Uncle Toby's wound in the groin to little Tristram's accident with the window later in the story. At this period jokes on all aspects of sex, including castration, were common enough, but Sterne seems to dwell on the idea at unusual length.**

After his fiasco with the forceps, which does nothing to alleviate Mr. Shandy's anxiety, the doctor goes upstairs to see what can be done. Walter exclaims that it is only two hours and ten minutes since the arrival of Dr. Slop, but it seems like an age. As we know by now, any remark like this, made by himself or others, sends Walter Shandy off into a fit of philosophical speculation, and the present occasion is no exception. Toby surprises him by saying that the idea of time is all due to the succession of ideas. His brother is relieved to find, however, that Captain Toby does not know what his statement means, and thus his brother has the chance to explain it. Walter now propounds Locke's idea of duration; we have ideas in succession, and are aware that they come one after another. The conviction in our minds that we have an idea at one instant and a second one later on marks, so to speak, two different points in time. The practical Toby, however, protests that he can make nothing of all this.

CHAPTERS 20-25

Annoyed, Walter Shandy breaks off the discourse and stares into the fire, and before they know it both brothers are asleep. Now, says the author, all his major characters are otherwise occupied, and he has time to insert his Preface. It is addressed to all the Anti-Shandeans, and critics. The writer has used all the wit and judgment that he has in the writing of his book, and calls down from heaven a like amount, or more, of the same commodities for his critics. There is only a certain amount of wit and judgment available for everyone but since in Arctic regions these qualities would be entirely frozen and thus unnecessary for the inhabitants, there is some left over for more temperate islands such as Britain. The climate there, which changes so rapidly, produces sudden stimulation or inhibition of these creative faculties, which accounts for the sudden productiveness of one period and the barrenness of the succeeding one. As a matter of fact, Sterne says, his prayer for additional wit and judgment for his critics is only a polite **convention**, for the amount in reality is very strictly rationed. And heaven forbid that it should be otherwise, for if these qualities were more generally available, we would have people making decisions on sensible grounds - doctors feeling their patient's pulses instead of their purses, lawyers rejecting unjust cases - and where would the world be then? As for the clergy .... but here even Sterne backs down; the picture saddens him too much.

He illustrates the equal importance of wit and judgment by the two knobs at the top of his chair. They are both ornamental, both on the same level, and when one is taken off the whole appearance of the chair is spoiled. Yet this seemingly obvious point has evaded the wisest and gravest heads of his time, even the great philosopher John Locke, who emphasizes the importance of judgment and discounts wit.

Comment: We have here another example of Sterne playing, in a half serious, half-comic way, with one of the most important ideas of his age. The argument about the relative importance of wit and judgment, especially for literary composition, is central to eighteenth-century critical thinking. The empirical philosopher Thomas Hobbes, the author of the *Leviathan*, brings up the question in the 1660's, and a hundred and forty years later the Romantic poet William Wordsworth provides his own resolution in the 1801 "Preface" to his Lyrical Ballads. The debate is a complex one, but, generally speaking, wit is the inventive faculty, working to arrange the images provided by the imagination in artistic and beautiful patterns. Judgment is the selective and censoring agent, passing on the aptness and propriety of what the wit has generated. A great deal of what now seems pointless squabbling took place about which of the two was the more important. It now appears obvious that if we are to talk about poetic creation in these terms at all, the two faculties must be given equal weight. John Locke, in his attempt to provide

a rational answer for everything, naturally came down heavily on the side of judgment. Here we see the serious undertone to our author's resolutely whimsical work. Sterne realized that life cannot be explained, or lived, in terms of reason alone; the irrational side of life, which is expressed artistically by the wit, is equally important, and men neglect this side of their natures at their peril.

Events in the next few chapters hinge upon the fact that the parlor door squeaks. Corporal Trim comes in to show off two model cannon which he has made out of an old pair of boots, and wakes up the sleeping brothers. Walter is aghast to see the cannon, for the boots were family heirlooms, and takes the occasion to read Toby a lecture on the unreasonable expense he incurs with his mock battles, but the Captain's good humor soon smooths over the situation.

The house is so quiet that the expectant father asks Trim what is going on, and the Corporal replies that everyone is upstairs except the doctor, who is busy in the kitchen making a bridge. Uncle Toby assumes that he means a bridge across a river, and to explain how he could make this mistake the author takes up the tale of Toby's wooing of the widow Wadman, and Trim's adventure in connection with the affair.

Comment: Uncle Toby's courtship of the widow Wadman forms a persistent theme through *Tristram Shandy*, and furnishes most of the material for Book IX. Sterne, of course, exploits the shyness of the naive Captain for humorous effect, but also uses the occasion to introduce a number of sentimental touches.

Corporal Trim, who admires Uncle Toby and imitates him in everything, uses his master's pursuit of Mrs. Wadman as an excuse for doing some pursuing of his own. In his case the object is Bridget, the maid. Toby is repulsed, but Trim meets with better success, and has an opportunity one moonlit night to show Bridget around the model fortifications. During the excursion, it chances that Uncle Toby's drawbridge is broken down, which provides Walter with the opportunity to josh his brother about the Corporal's powers of destruction. Toby attempts to design a new bridge to replace the broken one, but his inventions are so elaborate that they cannot be built. When he hears that Dr. Slop is making a bridge, he assumes that his difficulty is solved.

CHAPTERS 26–30

The bridge, however, Walter learns to his horror, is a bridge for little Tristram's nose, which has been crushed flat by the doctor's forceps during delivery. This last blow is too much for the new father, and he is forced to lie down, while Toby tries to comfort him, but can think of nothing to say. Although Walter's philosophy should be a source of consolation to him, it also leaves him open to bitter disappointments. His preoccupation with the importance of noses makes this accident seem especially tragic.

CHAPTERS 31–35

The accident to Tristram's nose provides occasion for a great deal of speculation on noses in general. Tristram's great-grandmother drove a hard bargain with her future husband over the marriage settlement because that gentleman had an inconsiderable nose. The author warns that the word nose means nothing but what it does mean, and is not to be interpreted as a polite disguise for any other organ. The prejudice of Tristram's father, then, in favor of long noses is deeply rooted, even an ancestral heritage.

Comment: Here, as elsewhere in the book, we must beware when Sterne specifically says things like the nose means nothing but what it does mean.

There is fear that Tristram will be castrated at birth, but only his nose is broken; his great-grandmother quibbled over her marriage settlement because her husband had an inconsiderable nose; a great number of "authorities" on the subject are discussed and the tale of Slawkenbergius is told. Later in the book, Tristram is actually "circumcised" by a falling window sash, and the identification between the male sex organ and the euphemistic nose is made clear: the accident feared at his birth and suffered only to his nose at that time has happened.

His father, Tristram comments, seizes hold of an idea and appropriates it for his own, refusing to let it go, in the same way that man in a state of nature picks up and claims for his own property an apple which he happens to find. The labor of picking up the apple, just like the mental effort expended in seizing the idea, makes it the legitimate possession of the finder.

Comment: The speculation and philosophical argument about "natural man" is the target of Sterne's wit here. The ideas of the French philosopher Jean Jacques Rousseau on this subject were gaining widespread attention at this time. To oversimplify Rousseau's ideas greatly, man in a state of nature had no property - and no vices. Civilization was a corrupting influence.

Here Tristram interrupts himself to pay tribute to Uncle Toby's goodness, in sentimental fashion. He then goes on to explain that one difficulty which lay in the way of his father's speculation on noses was the lack of learned treatises on the subject. He collected all he could find, but there were not many.

CHAPTERS 36–42

There is only a bare mention of long noses in the Renaissance philosopher Erasmus, though Walter turns and twists the text in trying to find more.

> **Comment: At this point Sterne inserts another of his jokes upon the reader. It is a marbled page, made of the specially decorated paper which was used for the end papers of books at that time. Without extensive reading, the author says, his audience will no more be able to understand the meaning of his book than of this marbled page, which is the "motley emblem of my work!" Motley, of course, refers to the parti-colored clothes which the court jesters used to wear, and thus a motley page is a fitting emblem for a jesting book.**

The most profuse and learned writer on long noses, Walter discovers, is the German philosopher Hafen Slawkenbergius, who has devoted his life to the subject. To buttress this authority Sterne invents a host of other experts on noses, all with impressive Latinized names, who have discoursed on the importance of long noses and the reason a man's nose should be long in the first place. The most convincing theory is that the infant's nose is crushed against its nurse's breast; to preserve and encourage the nose, then, a soft-breasted nurse should be chosen. Try as he will, however, Tristram's father cannot convince Uncle Toby of the importance of noses; arguments on the subject, marked by agitated explanation on Walter Shandy's side and placid resistance on Toby's, are responsible for a number of lively family scenes.

As an aid to logical argument, another concept borrowed from Locke makes its appearance here, the medius terminus, or intermediate idea. Two ideas which are so dissimilar that they cannot be compared directly can be dealt with by relating both to a third idea, the medius terminus. Sterne plays with this logical construction as he does continually with the mechanics of logic, by suggesting that the medius terminus in the argument between Tristram's father and Uncle Toby must be Uncle Toby's pipe, which the Captain is continually handling and measuring with his eye while his brother discourses on the length of noses. What especially annoys Walter, however, and drives him to all sorts of odd and fantastic gestures, is the quality of Toby's questions, derived as they are from equal parts of simplicity, absence of mind and plain inattention. Just as his brother thinks that he has explained everything in a splendidly rational way, Toby asks a question so wide of the mark that it is obvious he has not the faintest idea of what is going on. The solution of the problem of noses, for Uncle Toby, is perfectly simple: some noses are longer than others because God wishes it to be that way.

Sterne ends Book III with a final paean of praise for Slawkenbergius, and a promise to tell one of the tales from the German philosopher's work in his next volume.

Comment: The German philosopher Hafen Slawkenbergius is a complete fabrication of Sterne's, a point which some of the parson's contemporary readers missed. Literary hacks, taking advantage of the popularity of *Tristram Shandy*, dreamed up other treatises of Slawkenbergius and sometimes tried to pass them off as Sterne's own. Sterne intended the name Slawkenbergius to be a rude pun in German.

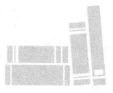

TRISTRAM SHANDY

. . . .

SLAWKENBERGIUS'S TALE

The author includes in his text a few pages of the Latin original; they appear side by side with the translation. The Latin work, he says, is exceedingly rare. The tale begins with the appearance one evening of a stranger at the town gate of Strasburg, a stranger with a wonderfully long nose. He carries a scimitar without a sheath just to protect this marvelous nose. To the innkeeper he explains that he has just returned from the Promontory of Noses, and has obtained there one of the best. All the townspeople speculate on whether this fantastic nose is real or not; the stranger will let no one touch it. The curiosity of the citizens is so great that the stranger becomes alarmed and rides on beyond the town before he stops for the night. Conjecture about the incredible nose throws the whole of Strasburg into an uproar; no one, clergy or laity, gets any sleep that night. All they know about the man is that he will return in a month's time.

The philosophers, doctors, lawyers, logicians, learned pedants of all kinds - none of them can think about anything else. The Strasburg universities, Lutheran and Catholic, happen at the time to be arguing about Martin Luther's damnation. The Catholics undertake to prove by astrology that he is inevitably damned, while the Lutherans say that their opponents have mistaken the date of his birth, and thus all their astrological calculations are incorrect. Actually, they say, he was born on the tenth of November, the eve of St. Martin's day, and derived his name of Martin in that way. At this point Tristram's father breaks in to point out to Toby how important names are, after all. In fact, Walter is so fond of this particular tale of Slawkenbergius because it deals with the two subjects of noses and names.

Even Martin Luther, however, is not enough to keep the faculties of the two universities away from the stranger's nose, and they divide into Nosarian and Antinosarian parties. The question now becomes theological: whether God could have made such an enormous nose. The Catholics are all for the unlimited power of God, including the power to make noses, while the Lutherans deny this as contrary to the natural order. As Sterne says here, "Heat [of speculation] is in proportion to the want of true knowledge."

Comment: Sterne is mocking the dual interests in theology and logical speculation which were popular at this time. This speculation led to such absurdities as, "Can God make two and two equal five?"

When the day set for the stranger's promised return arrives, all Strasburg sets out to meet him. A traveler now appears in search of the long-nosed stranger, whose name is Diego. He bears a message from his sister Julia, who had formerly rejected Diego and his nose, but now loves him. Diego immediately leaves the inn and returns to Julia, and the Strasburgers wait vainly for three days and nights upon the road. Their enemies the French, finding the city deserted, capture it, and the course of history is altered. It is easy to see from this tale, concludes Slawkenbergius, how important noses are in the world.

Comment: While the Shandean style is usually apt enough for Sterne's purposes, it is less successful in the case of a narrative like the one told by Slawkenbergius, which depends for its effect on a certain coherency of plot. In comparison with his philosophical asides, the author's attempt at story-telling seems only partially successful.

CHAPTERS 1–10

The author now proposes to continue with Slawkenbergius's next and final tale, but gives it up as untranslatable. Tristram's father is still prostrated by the shock of the accident to his son's nose, and remains so for an hour and a half, but at length the sight of Toby's sympathetic face stirs him to speech. Walter's comments on misfortune remind Corporal Trim of the sad fate of his brother Tom, a prisoner of the Inquisition, and the bad luck of former comrades-in-arms. All this moves Walter to reflect on the extraordinary way people survive in the face of misfortune. The human character can bear almost anything if there are good things to counterbalance the bad. The baby must have a superlative name to counteract his nose, and his father determines to name him Trismegistus. Toby philosophically points out that though things have been bad so far, they could be worse - the boy could have lost something even more important than his nose.

In Chapter 9, the writer points out, he has given us his promised chapter on chances, and Uncle Toby and his brother discuss these fortuitous accidents as they go down the stairs. In the tenth, we are presented with a chapter on chapters; Tristram explains that he draws a line across the page whenever he feels so inclined, and begins a new one: ".... is a man to follow rules - or rules to follow him?"

CHAPTERS 11-20

Trismegistus, Walter Shandy explains, was the greatest king, philosopher and priest in all history. At this moment the maid goes by, and the new father asks how his wife is. "As well as can be expected," Susannah replies, and goes on about her business. Toby and his brother agree that all the women in the house suddenly give themselves airs when one of their number is in labor. It gives them a sense of their own importance, as well it might.

We have reached, says Sterne, now speaking in his own person, the middle of the fourth volume, and this is only the first day of Tristram's life! There are still 364 days in Tristram's first year; at the present rate the author will never catch up with himself! On reflection, however, this is not such a bad state of affairs after all. At least there is no lack of material to write about, if only the supply of paper holds out.

Susannah comes hurrying in to tell Mr. Shandy that the child is in a fit and may not live through the hour. What name should they use to christen him? The father, who has gone to bed by this time, gropes in the dark for his breeches and tells Susannah, "Trismegistus." Off rushes the maid to tell the curate who is about to baptize the child that the name is to be "Tris - something"; she has forgotten the rest. The curate declares that the name must be Tristram and Tristram the child is christened forthwith. Just as the ceremony is over, the father arrives on the scene, holding up his breeches with one hand.

A chapter on sleep would come in conveniently here, says Tristram, but the subject is too difficult. He must settle for a simpler one - on buttonholes, for instance, but he immediately proceeds to give us all the **cliches** and hackneyed sayings on the subject of sleep which he can remember.

The next morning Walter Shandy and Toby are settling down to a comfortable breakfast when the news is brought to them that the child has not been named Trismegistus, but Tristram. The disappointed father does not give violent vent to his feelings, but walks quietly out to look at his fish pond, which seems to be a soothing object. On his return he declares, in a crushed voice, that there is no use in struggling against destiny. The fates seem universally aligned against his son. Uncle Toby suggests that they send for Parson Yorick.

In the twentieth chapter we hear how the writer has gone riding hither and yon, dashing up, down, and across the highway, but without doing anyone any harm. Yes, he argues with himself, but this slap-dash riding jostles all kinds of important people out of the way, kings included. No matter for that, is the reply, on with the story.

Comment: This especially disorganized and Shandean chapter seems to have no purpose except to bring up the subject of kings as a preparation for the anecdote about a king in the next chapter.

CHAPTERS 21-25

A story is now told of King Francis the First of France, who decides to undertake a little international diplomacy by giving the republic of Switzerland the honor of standing godfather to his next child. A republic is a female creature, however, so Francis hastily asks the nation to be godmother instead. To this Switzerland happily agrees, but on condition that the Swiss be allowed to name the child. The king is ready to agree to this request as long as the name chosen is a reasonable one, but when he hears that they have hit upon Shadrach, Meshach, Abednego, he hastily calls off the negotiations. France has no money to pay Switzerland in order to smooth over the insult, and the king decides the only remedy is to go to war.

Comment: Why Sterne should insert this story at its present position in the book is something of a puzzle. The mention of kings in the previous chapter gives some slight starting point, and the story does revolve about names and christenings, but aside from these points the placement of the tale seems accidental. As a general rule, Sterne's digressions are very often connected, sometimes by rather subtle associations of ideas, with the events of his major plot, the history of young Tristram. He talks about sleep, for instance, because Walter Shandy has just been roused from it. But we should also bear in mind that Sterne had committed himself to turn out two volumes a year, and he usually left far too little time to do the job in a leisurely way. The style is not only intentionally jumbled, it is also very uneven, and sometimes Sterne's powers of invention flag badly.

In the next chapter we are told that the author has no intention of satirizing particular persons; the characters of the story are not famous people whose names have been disguised. "If 'tis wrote against anything," he says, "tis wrote against the spleen!"

> **Comment: By eighteenth-century definitions "the spleen" was a mixture of melancholy, boredom and anger which visited a man predisposed to this affliction at unpredictable times. The English as a nation considered themselves particularly cursed with the spleen, as a result of their Germanic heritage and the changeable weather. It was even referred to by foreigners as the "English sickness." *Tristram Shandy* is exactly the kind of book which makes an excellent remedy against the spleen; Sterne's claim that he is attacking the disease is a just one.**

It now appears that a great dinner is to be held in the city (the author ingenuously disguises the name as ****, by which all his contemporary readers knew he meant York) and Walter Shandy proposes to ask some of the learned men there whether his son's christening can be revoked and the name changed.

Chapter 24 is left out of the book entirely at this point, but the author assures us that it is an intentional omission, and no fault of the bookbinder. Walter Shandy refuses to travel in the coach, because the family coat-of-arms on the door has been painted incorrectly, so the Shandy party starts off for York on horse-back. Now the picture of this procession which made up Chapter 24 was so finely painted, says Tristram, that it depreciated every other scene in the book, and so for the sake of uniformity it was taken out. Sterne rounds out his remarks by making some sly hits at clerics who introduce quotations into their sermons. There is great danger that the quotation, if it is well written, will only show up the dullness of the rest of the sermon.

CHAPTERS 26–32

The opening of Chapter 26 finds the two Shandys and Parson Yorick at the great dinner at York, after having listened to the parson preach in the Cathedral. Yorick cuts up the sermon he has just preached into strips for lighting pipes, and Didius, one of the other diners, protests at this disrespectful treatment of something to which they have listened in good faith. The whimsical parson explains that the sermon has come from the head rather than the heart, and for this reason he is displeased with it. The conversation is interrupted by an exclamation of "Zounds!" from Phutatorius, who is sitting across the table from Toby. The company is surprised at this interruption, but it soon becomes clear that Phutatorius is not taking part in the attack on Yorick. A hot chestnut out of a supply just brought in by the waiter has fallen into Phutatorius' breeches, and the exclamation is one of surprise and pain. The surprised diner quickly fishes out the uncomfortable object and drops it on the floor, where Yorick picks it up.

Comment: The events of this dinner are based loosely on those of a real one which Sterne attended at York. The group was assembled to settle a dispute which had arisen between Dr. Francis Topham, a lawyer who transacted some of the official Cathedral business, on one side, and Sterne and the Dean of York Cathedral on the other. Dr. Topham is satirized under the names of both Didius and Phutatorius in the book. It appears that the lawyer was exceptionally greedy about collecting minor church offices with a salary attached to them. At one point in his machinations he refused an unimportant position in the hope of receiving a more lucrative one. When his larger hopes did not materialize, he reapplied for the smaller office, only to

find it had been given to Laurence Sterne! The accident of the chestnut is a humorous allegory of these events; Yorick picks it up because "he thought the chestnut not a jot the worse for the adventure," just as Sterne accepted the office without worrying about the fact that someone else had previously refused it.

The expression "Zounds!" is a contraction of the old medieval oath, "By God's wounds!" an example of the medieval habit of swearing by the attributes of Christ. It was still considered rather strong language in the eighteenth century, especially for use in a group which included clergymen.

Phutatorius, who is no friend of Yorick's to begin with, immediately suspects that the parson himself must have planted the chestnut. Of course Yorick is completely innocent. All his life, the author interjects, Yorick has been unfairly accused of just such "ungracious pranks," and it is really not in his nature to do anything of the sort. It is clear here that Sterne is talking of himself and the similar accusations made against him.

The question of Tristram's defective baptism, and the possibility of its annulment, is now put before the assembly. There is much learned argument about the words used in baptizing the child and its relationship to its mother (in law, declare these experts, it is no relation at all), but the dinner finally ends without coming to any decision upon Mr. Shandy's problem.

Comment: The "expert" is a favorite target of Sterne's satire. It will be remembered that the Doctors of the Sorbonne were unable to come to any conclusion on a similar problem earlier in the book. It is worth noticing that one of John Locke's avowed purposes in

writing the Essay Concerning Human Understanding was to deflate the charlatans and mock-philosophers who indulged in pompous speculation without any basis for their conjectures. Here it seems that Sterne has made Locke's enemies his own.

Although the speculation delights him, Tristram's father is plunged into gloom by the thought that there seems no way to relieve his son of his undesirable name. He is solaced, however, by a legacy of a thousand pounds from the self-willed Aunt Dinah who married the coachman. Walter is in a quandary over whether to use the money to send Tristram's elder brother Bobby on the Grand Tour, or to reclaim an unused piece of land belonging to the family, called the Ox-moor.

Comment: The "Grand Tour," of France, Italy and other countries of Western Europe, usually in the company of a tutor, was considered a necessary part of a well-to-do young man's education in Sterne's time. As the English poet Alexander Pope points out in his Dunciad, the youth was often "educated" in just those subjects his family would have wished him to avoid. The capacity for education of these sprigs of the nobility can also be deduced from the fact that their tutors were usually called "bear-leaders."

Mr. Shandy is rescued from his dilemma by Bobby's timely death, and the Ox-moor claims his attention; he has been engaged in an expensive lawsuit about it, and thus it is closer to his heart. Tristram, of course, becomes the heir of the Shandy family and fortunes, such as they are.

Comment: The exaggerated hopes of Tristram's father after he has cleared the Ox-moor and planted

crops on it are an ironic reflection of Sterne's own experiments in this direction. Sterne and his wealthy neighbors enclosed a large piece of common land in their parish and the parson spent considerable sums in trying to reclaim his portion. Although his expectations were as great as Mr. Shandy's, he was disappointed; his investment turned out to be money thrown down the drainage ditch.

In the last chapter of Book IV the author complains that he has not been able to talk about half of the things he wished to cover. He promises any number of good things for the next two volumes, for in them Tristram's career, properly speaking, will begin. After deliberately whetting his audience's appetite in this way, he bids them a polite farewell until next year "unless this vile cough kills me in the meantime."

Comment: Sterne's talk about coughs was no joke. His bouts with tuberculosis were becoming more serious at this time, especially since he exhausted himself first by writing and then with the frenzied social life of a literary lion in London.

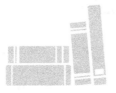

TRISTRAM SHANDY

BOOK V

. . . .

CHAPTERS 1–10

At the beginning of *Tristram Shandy*, when Sterne was still an unknown writer, he contented himself with a mock inscription, in the middle of the volume, offering to dedicate the book to anyone willing to pay for the privilege. Now, as an established and even famous author, he can afford the prestige of a genuine dedication to an important person, and Volumes V and VI are prefaced by a flattering letter to John, Viscount Spencer.

Comment: Sterne's dedication to Lord Spencer was the occasion of an amusing sally by Samuel Johnson, the famous lexicographer and literary arbiter. "In a company where I lately was," says Johnson, "Tristram Shandy introduced himself; and Tristram Shandy had scarcely sat down, when he informed us that he had been writing a Dedication to Lord Spencer; and sponte sua [of his own free will] he pulled it out of

his pocket; and sponte sua, for nobody desired him, he began to read it; and before he had read half a dozen lines, sponta mea [of my own free will], sir, I told him it was not English, sir." Johnson may have found Sterne's grammar disturbing enough, but he found the bawdy stories the clergyman told during the course of the evening even worse. Apparently the two never met again.

Book V begins with a Shandean rhapsody upon the difficulty of writing, and the near-impossibility of adding anything to the real stock of learning. This leads him, by a connection which he leaves the reader to guess, to the subject of whiskers. A fragmentary story about Queen Margaret of Navarre and her court now follows, in which the word "whiskers" becomes a synonym for a much less mentionable part of the anatomy. The author points out how even the best word can become corrupted by associating it with improper ideas.

Comment: The story of the Queen of Navarre is supposed to be illustrative of the subject of whiskers just as Slawkenbergius's tale deals with the subject of noses. The present tale, however, is a great deal less effective, being entirely devoid of plot and hingeing for its effect on a single bawdy joke. Sterne is in no position to complain, as he does, about other people corrupting words; he himself constantly makes use of indecent double-entendres.

Returning to the Shandy household at last, we find Tristram's father calculating the expense of his eldest son Bobby's travels through Europe. Since horses and coach have to be paid for by the mile, the computation is a delicate task involving much point-to-point measurement on the map. He is interrupted, losing his place each time, first by the entrance of the servant Obadiah to ask if he can use the coach-horse, and then by the arrival of a letter, which he gives to Toby to read. The letter contains the news of Bobby's death. Mr. Shandy is so eccentric that he reacts to nothing in the ordinary way. Now, instead of bursting into tears, he is comforted by the thought of the enormous amount of rhetoric which has been expended on the subject of death. Quotation after quotation comes into his head, and he proceeds to patch together a funeral oration on the spot. The references to classical times and persons confuse Toby, who thinks that his brother is talking about his own experiences.

> **Comment: Walter Shandy's philosophical reflections upon death are borrowed wholesale from the Elizabethan author Robert Burton's *Anatomy of Melancholy*, a favorite book of Sterne's.**

A curious fact about the Shandy household is that all the actions and conversations which take place in the parlor have their parallels in the kitchen, among the servants. There the news of young master Bobby's death inspires Trim to a funeral oration, and awakens a train of ideas in each of the other servants' minds.

> **Comment: This passage, in which Sterne shows how each member of the group reacts in a different way to the same event, is a clever piece of mass characterization. Here the author uses Locke's theories about the association of ideas for his own purposes; he shows that the reaction of each member of the household to the news is connected with his or her personality.**

Susannah, the maid, can only think that her mistress will no longer need all her fine clothes, now that she is going into mourning. The scullion, who has been ill, rejoices that it is someone else who is dead, and not herself. Obadiah foresees that now the Ox-moor will be cultivated in earnest, which means more work for him.

Corporal Trim's oration is as rhetorical, in its unliterary way, as Walter's, and a good deal more dramatic. "Are we not here now, and are we not" he says, dropping his hat to the ground, "gone in a moment?" All the servants find this visual effect particularly striking, and Susannah bursts into tears. In this sentimental vein Trim goes on for a good while, and concludes that his master, Captain Toby, will take the loss hardest, for he has the tenderest heart and cannot, like his brother, console himself with words. The melancholy events bring to the Corporal's mind the story of one of Toby's friends in the Army, Lieutenant Le Fever.

CHAPTERS 11–20

The next few chapters, very short ones, are unusually full of Shandean digressions - on the life of Socrates, the quality of truth, the geographical transmission of ideas and the curiosity of women. The last subject arises because Mrs. Shandy is listening at the parlor door to her husband's funeral oration, her attention having been attracted by the word "wife." Mr. Shandy has just quoted Socrates' statement that he had three children when Tristram's mother breaks in to ask where this new member of the household has appeared from so suddenly. Uncle Toby reassures her that the reference is to Socrates' children, not her own.

When the household has settled down after its bereavement, Mr. Shandy sets out to write up a system of education for his remaining son, which he calls his Trista-paedia.

Comment: The Greek word paedia used as a suffix means pertaining to education; the great classical books on education contain the word in their titles. Sterne refers particularly here to the Greek historian Xenophon's Cyropaedia, written for the instruction of the young man who was to become Cyrus the Great, King of Persia.

As we have seen, Tristram's father is a pedantic soul, and he becomes so absorbed and involved in his subject that his son has already outgrown the first part of the book before it is completed. In fact, there is danger of Mr. Shandy forgetting about Tristram entirely, except that an accident to the boy again makes him the center of attention. Because of the absence of a chamber pot (Sterne disguises the offensive name with *****) Susannah hoists young Tristram to the window sill so that he can relieve himself out the window (again concealed by *****). The window, which is badly hung, suddenly comes crashing down, and poor Tristram suffers an unexpected circumcision. The maid, in terror, flees to Toby's house and tells Trim the bad news. The Corporal is as disturbed as Susannah because he is an accessory - he "borrowed" the lead sash weights to make model cannon for Toby's fortifications.

CHAPTERS 21-30

Trim bravely takes the blame for Tristram's accident, and reports the affair to his master. Toby is talking to Yorick, and is, as usual, giving a description of one of King William's battles. The Corporal adds his own eyewitness account of the engagement, thus proving that he is brave enough for the task before him. Then Toby, Yorick, Trim and Susannah go off in military order to carry the bad news to Tristam's father. As Sterne puts it, "without either drums beating, or colors flying, they marched slowly from my uncle Toby's house to Shandy-hall." As we have seen already, Walter Shandy's reactions are not like those of ordinary men, and are utterly unpredictable. Little Tristram's yells have attracted his mother and the servants, and the household is soon well informed about the nature of his misfortune. When he is told the news, Mr. Shandy's only comment is, "I thought as much." Toby's peace mission, when it arrives, at least does not have the embarrassing task of breaking the news.

Tristram's father arrives at his son's bedside, only to turn and go downstairs again. His wife imagines that he has gone for bandages, but he returns carrying a couple of books. They are not medical manuals, but treatises on the laws of the Hebrews, and he consults this authority to find out the possible advantages of circumcision! He finds additional comfort in the fact that the Egyptians, Syrians, Phoenicians and many other nations of antiquity approved of the practice. When Yorick appears, Walter complains humorously that his son seems to have unusual difficulty with religious rituals, from christening on.

Seeing that all his friends have assembled, Mr. Shandy seizes the opportunity to read to them out of the educational system he has been writing for his son, the Trista-paedia. Though the work has been slow, he has made some progress, and he proposes that this be the first of a series of readings from the book.

CHAPTERS 31-43

The Trista-paedia begins by attempting to prove that the conjunction of the male and female is the basis of society. The author's approach is nothing if not theoretical, and he continues with a discussion of the natural relation between father and child.

Uncle Toby objects that some of the rules which he derives from obscure authorities can be found just as well in the Catechism, and adds proudly that Trim can recite the whole thing. He is obviously anxious to have someone question the Corporal on the subject, and Yorick obliges by asking Trim the Fifth Commandment. The ex-soldier replies that he cannot answer when the question is put in that way. The Catechism is like the manual of arms; you must begin at the beginning and proceed straight on, by the numbers. Toby puts him through his paces, and he both performs the manual of arms and barks out the Commandments with military precision. Walter Shandy, who has been watching all this with amusement, comments, "Everything in this world is big with jest - and has wit in it, and instruction too - if we can but find it out."

Comment: This statement makes a perfect motto for *Tristram Shandy*. It reflects Laurence Sterne's attitude that anything at all can be treated humorously, and provides us with his own reason for writing the book. He wanted first to see the fun in the world, but also, secondarily, to draw "instruction," from it, especially from his myriad accounts of human folly.

Mr. Shandy goes on to demonstrate in the Trista-paedia that good health is entirely dependent on the proper mixture of radical heat and radical moisture. He clinches his point with attacks upon the Greek physician Hippocrates and the Elizabethan statesman and essayist Francis Bacon, Lord Verulam, both of whose systems of treatment he discounts entirely.

Comment: The concepts of radical heat and radical moisture as supporters of health within the body formed part of a well-known and widely accepted theory of physiology - but at this time the theory was about a hundred years out of date.

Toby listens with great interest to this description, and comments that the most radical and healthful moisture he knows of was the spiced brandy and good Geneva gin drunk, while the Army was encamped in the open, to keep off fever and ague. The captain is about to launch into an account of the bouts with fever which he and Trim survived at the siege of Limerick, when Dr. Slop walks in. The doctor describes little Tristram's condition in terms that no one understands. Then Trim is asked his own opinion of radical heat and radical moisture. The Corporal, drawing analogies from the siege of Limerick, concludes that radical moisture is ditchwater, with which they were practically inundated during the siege, and that radical heat must be the antidote of which they availed themselves, burnt brandy.

Returning to his book of instruction, Tristram's father is concerned about the length of time spent in educating the child. He is convinced that there must be some short cut to education, "a North-west passage to the intellectual world."

Comment: Mariners and explorers had been looking since the discovery of the New World for a shorter western passage to China and India which would eliminate the hazardous journey around Cape Horn. "A North-west passage" had become a synonym for some long desired but seemingly unattainable goal.

Mr. Shandy decides that the key to the whole matter must lie in the auxiliary verbs. According to him, improvisation, speculation, and the construction of **metaphors** are the highest goals of education, and all these involve the use of the auxiliaries. Make the child master of these verbs and he is competent in any subject. In the middle of this train of thought; and quite without warning, Book V ends.

TRISTRAM SHANDY

BOOK VI

CHAPTERS 1–10

The author congratulates himself and his readers for having got through the wilderness of the five previous volumes. He is especially impressed by the number of jackasses in the world, and by their reception of his book: "How they viewed and reviewed us...." The reader has a strong suspicion that the jackasses in question are the reviewers and critics, especially those who do not like *Tristram Shandy*.

Tristram's father is convinced that by his method of education his son will quickly become a prodigy of learning, and he goes on to rhapsodize about the astonishing children of the past. While this is going on, Dr. Slop and Susannah are attempting to bandage Tristram, but the maid's modesty prevents her from being very helpful.

Walter Shandy feels it high time to obtain a tutor for his son (Sterne calls him a "governor"). He requires such enormous learning and perfection of temperament from a tutor that it seems unlikely one will ever be found, but Toby recommends the son of his old Army friend, Le Fever. The mention of his name provides an excuse for the author to tell the sad tale of Le Fever.

Captain Toby is one day sitting at supper when the landlord of a local inn comes in to ask for some wine for a sick soldier who is staying with him. The Captain sends Trim to find out who the man is, and discovers that he is an unfortunate lieutenant, prevented by illness from joining his regiment. The lieutenant's son, a boy of eleven or twelve, is attempting to take care of his father. Toby and Corporal Trim show the goodness of their hearts by offering to do everything they can to help the luckless pair. Le Fever's wife, it appears, was killed by a musket shot as she lay in his arms, during the campaign of Breda.

The Captain even reproaches his servant for not having offered Le Fever the use of his house and money as well. He determines that he will take care of the sick man himself; in a few weeks they will have him healthy again and marching back to his regiment. Trim objects that the sick lieutenant will never march again, except into his grave, but his master insists that he will, he must, recover.

"He shall not die, by G-,' cried my uncle Toby. The Accusing Spirit, which flew up to heaven's chancery with the oath, blushed as he gave it in, - and the Recording Angel, as he wrote it down, dropped a tear upon the word, and blotted it out forever."

Comment: The story of Le Fever, and in particular the portion of it just quoted, was the part of Book VI most admired by Sterne's contemporaries. It is an exercise

in sentimental writing, a genre at which the author was very skillful. One of the most important reasons for the immediate success of *Tristram Shandy* was the accuracy with which Sterne gauged the public appetite for the pathetic, for the kind of writing which aroused pity as the principal emotion in its readers. While Laurence Sterne cannot be called the inventor of the vogue of sentiment, he was enormously influential in popularizing the form. Early critics gave him credit for coining the word "sentimental," though it now appears that others had preceded him. Even if he was not the inventor of the word, he was the one who made it widely known. He is the predecessor of such important figures in the history of literary taste as Henry Mackenzie (1745–1831), whose *Man of Feeling* (1771) is pointed to as one of the first novels to derive its appeal almost entirely from the exploitation of sentimentality.

The Captain goes to see Le Fever the next morning to present him with the offer of lodging and care, but this kindness is only just in time to lighten the last few minutes of the lieutenant's life. Le Fever's death is described in another sentimental passage.

CHAPTERS 11–20

Parson Yorick preaches a sermon at the funeral, and provides an opportunity for the author to make a few comments on sermons and their writers. Most preachers, he remarks, note at the head of their sermons the time, place and occasion when they are preached, with comments about their suitability, Biblical source, and in some cases the place where most of the sermon was "borrowed" from.

Comment: Sterne can describe this practice because it is exactly what he did himself. A good many of his own sermons were reworkings of earlier ones by famous preachers.

Some of Yorick's sermons are marked "So, so," others "moderato," and others "lentamente," "tenute" and "adagio." These musical terms are evidently Yorick's whimsical way of describing the pace of the sermon, and at the same time expressing his opinion of it. At the end of the funeral sermon for Le Fever, for example, he has written, "Bravo!" However, the word is written in such exceedingly small letters, and in such very pale ink, that it would be unfair to accuse the parson of self-congratulation. Besides all this, the word is crossed out.

The kind-hearted Toby takes charge of young Le Fever's education, but the boy only stays in school until the age of seventeen. At that time he returns to Captain Shandy, asks for the lieutenant's sword which Toby has kept for him, and sets out for the wars to follow his father's profession. The young man's career, in spite of his bravery, is dogged by misfortune, and sickness causes his return to England just in time to be proposed as young Tristram's tutor.

In a fashion typical of Sterne, the story now goes off in an entirely different direction. Dr. Slop, to enhance his own reputation for wonderful cures, has spread the tale that young Tristram was completely castrated by the window. His father, in an effort to squelch this rumor, determines to put the boy into breeches, thus affirming the masculinity of his son.

Comment: At this time very young children of both sexes were clothed in a kind of dress or tunic. The day when a boy was "put into breeches," usually

around the age of seven, was a proud occasion for both parents and son, marking, as it did, the boy's entry into the masculine world.

Although Mr. Shandy's decision seems to have been made on the spur of the moment, it is actually the result of much reflection and consultation, particularly in two "beds of justice" which he has held. Tristram's father seems to feel that if judicial proceedings are called a court of justice because they are held in a building called a court, then the serious consultation between husband and wife which takes place in bed should be called a "bed of justice." Like the ancient Goths who argued every question twice, once drunk and once sober, Walter Shandy is careful to debate every question in two different states of mind, and to settle on some plan which strikes a balance between the two different attitudes thus produced. Tristram varies the formula by doing half his writing after a good dinner and the other half when he is hungry. In this way, he says, he strikes such a happy balance between impulse and discretion that "I write a careless kind of a civil, nonsensical, good-humored Shandean book, which will do all your hearts good. -And all your heads too - provided you understand it."

Comment: Sterne always insisted, at least partly with tongue in cheek, we must suspect, that his books were meant to improve as well as amuse.

Chapter 18 gives us some of these "beds of justice," word for word, in which Walter Shandy discusses the subject of breeches. Mrs. Shandy agrees with every word that her husband says, no matter how contradictory his statements are, or how much he may actually be wishing for a negative answer. (Tristram says near the beginning of *Tristram Shandy* that the women in his family had "no character at all") Mr. Shandy gives up in disgust because he can get nothing but agreeable responses from his wife, and turns to one of his ancient authorities, Albertus Rubenius. That learned man, however, though he enumerates and describes every kind of classical garment imaginable, nowhere mentions breeches. Tristram's father fastens on one article of dress worn by the ancients which Rubenius mentions, the latus clavus. Though his authority is unable to define the term, Mr. Shandy deduces that it refers to hooks and eyes, and so Tristram's first breeches are made with hooks and eyes under his father's personal supervision.

Now, says the author, let us dismiss the tailor, making the breeches with Walter standing over him, let us dismiss Mrs. Shandy, and Dr. Slop, and poor young Le Fever, and shift to a new scene of events. It would be best of all if we could leave the author himself behind, he adds, but that is impossible.

CHAPTERS 21-30

The new scene in which we find ourselves is Uncle Toby's bowling green, the place where the ex-soldier reconstructs the fortified towns of Europe and re-enacts their sieges. When the fortification itself is done, they begin to construct the parallels, and go through all the stages of the siege. The Captain follows, with the closest attention. the campaigns of the Duke of Marlborough, as detailed in the newspapers and periodicals dealing with military affairs, and every move the Duke makes is mimicked on the bowling green.

Comment: John Churchill, Duke of Marlborough, and one of England's most illustrious generals, led the armies of "the Grand Alliance" (principally composed of England, Holland and Austria) against Louis XIV of France and his allies. The battles which Toby Shandy

recreated on his bowling green were a part of the war which began in 1690 and did not end until the Treaty of Utrecht in 1713. Actually, there were two wars (referred to in America as "King William's War" and "Queen Anne's War") separated by the peace of Ryswick (1697–1701). The Siege of Namur, in which Toby suffered his wound, occurred in 1694.

A number of eighteenth-century writers, among them Joseph Addison in his Spectator and Daniel Defoe, the author of Robinson Crusoe, made fun of the people who waited breathlessly for every piece of news from abroad. At this time newspapers and periodicals devoted to news (often called gazettes) were becoming increasingly popular, and there were groups of men who spent hours in the coffeehouses in order to pick up and discuss the latest dispatch from the Continent. Sterne is making fun of the same exaggerated interest, but, in the case of Uncle Toby, in a much gentler way. Toby's hobby-horse is an example of the "ruling passion" at work; it is another serious idea that Sterne treats in a comic way. Giving way to one's ruling passion is supposed to lead to disaster, but the "hobby-horse" solaces the old soldier's declining years and brings nothing but happiness to him and Corporal Trim.

"Parallels" are the trenches dug parallel to the walls of a city to shelter the troops engaged in the siege.

As the years go by the Captain makes more and more improvements in his military establishment; he adds drawbridges, gates with portcullises, a sentry-box, and finally a whole model town, made of separate houses, which can be arranged in the exact pattern of the real town under siege. From here they progress to a church to ornament the town, complete with steeple, brass cannon, and various other sorts of artillery, including the pieces made from the Shandy family jack boots. It is lucky for the Shandys and their neighbors that the cannon are not strong enough to take gunpowder, but Toby is perplexed about how he is to reproduce the effect of firing. Trim, however, swears that he will find some way out of this difficulty.

The next morning Uncle Toby prepares himself for the most important siege of the campaign, dressing himself up with unusual care. When he arrives at the fortification, he finds Trim has preceded him. At this point Sterne breaks off to write an apostrophe on Trim's genius, and to mourn his death, and that of Toby himself. Despite the confusion of time that is involved here, the passage is an evocative one, another successful exercise is the sentimental genre.

Trim has availed himself of two Turkish waterpipes sent home by his brother from the East. By means of some interconnecting piping, he attaches the pipes to his six cannon, and when Toby arrives they are smoking away in fine fashion. Even though the thing is beneath his dignity, the Captain cannot bear to let his servant have all the fun, and is soon in possession of one of the pipes, smoking away as hard as Trim.

Now, says the author, he will proceed to exhibit Toby in a new character. What distinguishes the Captain is an extraordinary simplicity and naivete in all non-military matters, and a corresponding ignorance of the wiles of women. Added to this is the complete modesty of his nature. Among the few men who are immune to, or perhaps simply unacquainted with, love, military heroes form the largest number, and Toby has so far been among them.

CHAPTERS 31–40

The Treaty of Utrecht (1713) comes near to breaking Toby's heart since it puts an end to all the sieges he is so fond of following. When his brother teases him about the loss of his hobby-horse, he becomes indignant, and for Toby, eloquent. Chapter 32 is devoted to his "Apologetical Oration," which Walter copied down and Tristram found among his papers.

Comment: This sense of the word "apology" means a defense or explanation, not an excuse.

The Captain admits that from childhood the sound of drum and trumpet excited him as nothing else could. But he is as aware of the evils of war, of towns destroyed and children orphaned, as any philanthropist. It is one thing to stand in the front rank of battle and act the hero's part, and quite another to reflect upon the consequence of those acts and upon the miserable life of the private soldier, taken as a whole. Besides, some people are created to fight, just as others are fitted for gentler occupations. What is war, after all, "but the getting together of quiet and harmless people, with their swords in their hands, to keep the ambitious and turbulent within bounds?"

Comment: Sterne presents here one of the standard eighteenth-century rationales for war, and at the same time gives us a kind of philosophical basis for the portrait he has drawn throughout the book of Toby as the gentle soldier. The apparent contradiction between the gentleness of his nature and the harshness of his profession provides a piquancy to the character sketch of the retired Captain which the author is well aware of, and at the

same time makes the picture an appropriate one to hang in his gallery of "sentimental" characters.

The Peace of Utrecht calls for the demolition of the fortified town of Dunkirk, and this seems almost the only kind of military work left for Toby and Trim. Peace negotiations, however, are so much slower than warfare that it takes months even for these conditions to be confirmed, and in the meantime the two are left in a fatal idleness. The Captain's attention is insensibly drawn from the arts of war to those of love, from the soldier's trumpet to the lover's lute.

The author spends an entire short chapter (Chapter 36) saying that he will not give a theoretical description of what love is, nor quote a hundred learned authorities, as his father would have done. By Chapter 37, he gets around to telling us in plain language that Uncle Toby fell in love. This fact is not surprising, Sterne assures us, because the reader has never seen anyone as beautiful as the object of his love, the widow Wadman.

To imagine her properly, says the author, we must draw her ourselves, and he conveniently leaves a blank page for the reader to do just that. We can use our imaginations, he adds, making her as like our mistresses or unlike our wives as we wish. There, he concludes, after the blank page, is one page of the book which no reader will criticize!

The women, of course, know all about this affair long before Toby is aware of it himself. Mrs. Shandy tells her husband that her brother and the widow are to be married, but as usual she simply agrees with all the comments which he makes on the matter. At this point Tristram interrupts to say that he has got well into the story, and should now be able to proceed in a straight line. He then draws a series of wiggly lines in the text, with lots of offshoots and digressions, and explains that these are the lines that he moved through in the first five volumes. In the last volume he has done better; from the end of Le Fever's story to the beginning of Uncle Toby's campaigns he has digressed very little. At this rate, he will soon be able to proceed in this way - and he draws a perfectly straight line. This is the line, he insists, which has been called the proper path for Christians to walk, the favorite of the geometricians, and the only sensible way to plant cabbages. But why has this been called the line of gravitation, he asks. The clear implication is that such a line need not be grave; it can be as funny as any other.

TRISTRAM SHANDY

TEXTUAL ANALYSIS

BOOK VII

. . . .

CHAPTERS 1–10

Tristram reminds the reader that he has promised to write two volumes a year, provided his terrible cough will permit him.

Luckily his spirits remain good, though his health is bad. In fact, when Death himself knocked at his door, he was able to answer so cheerfully that Death thought he had mistaken the address. Now he proposes to fly to France, where Death may not follow him, and by the end of the first chapter we find him at Dover.

Comment: All the jokes which Sterne makes about imminent death are a very real reflection of the true situation. He did go to France to see if he would benefit from the better climate, but the improvement in his health was only a temporary one.

He is very seasick on the passage, and glad to get ashore, but when he gets there he is confronted with the problem of which route to take to Paris. Most travelers stop and give their readers an account of every large town they pass, but Tristram confesses that since he arrived in Calais late in the evening and left before dawn in the morning, he saw very little of it. Nevertheless, he adds, he can probably give as good a description of it as most travel writers, and in Chapter 5 he proceeds to do so. The chapter is a very funny **parody** of travel-book writing, in which the author keeps making pointless observations about the features of the town, all obviously derived from hearsay, and drawing totally unnecessary conclusions. He points out, as an especially curious fact, that the weakest part of the town is the most heavily fortified. The church steeple is supported by four pillars, "elegant and light enough, but sufficiently strong at the same time." The resemblance here, even to modern guide-books, is unmistakable.

However, the author says, he scorns to impose any more of this stuff on his loyal and long-suffering readers. Instead, he continues with an account of his journey, in which he hurries on so fast that all the bystanders wonder what he can be fleeing. They speculate about the police, but we know that his pursuer is Death. His carriage is always breaking down upon the road, but unlike other travelers, who curse the gods and write scathing denunciations of the French system of transportation, he accepts the delay philosophically and contrives to make reasonable progress by dint of small bribes to the driver. What he describes are not the monuments and points of historical interest; these will always be there for the reader to see for himself. Instead he will depict the small details of human behavior, which are far more interesting to him as illustrations of human nature. Unlike the monuments, these may be gone in an hour. As we know by now, when Sterne speaks of human nature he has in mind as often as not a pretty girl, and he gives us a charming portrait of Janatone, the innkeeper's daughter at Montreuil.

CHAPTERS 11–20

In Chapter 12 Sterne returns to the subject of death, and remarks that he would rather meet it in a decent inn, among strangers, than at home, surrounded by friends.

> Comment: Whether the author is sincere in these remarks or not, the circumstances of his death were strangely like those he describes here. He died in lodgings in London (his wife and daughter were in France), attended only by a hired nurse and a servant whom his friends had sent to inquire after his health. It is odd that this man, whose books are full of sentiment and sentimentality, should at this last juncture reject these qualities.

> As Sterne's health worsened and the pressure of having to publish each year became more of a burden, the chapters of *Tristram Shandy* got shorter and shorter. In this volume many of them take up no more than a page and the style becomes even more disjointed than usual. It should also be noted that although it is ostensibly Tristram who is traveling in France, Sterne speaks more and more in his own person, giving a version of his own travels on the Continent and reflecting his own interests and point of view. The preoccupation with people rather than places, for instance, is a reflection of Sterne's personal attitude.

In this especially Shandean portion of the book, the author goes off into a dissertation on the size of souls (they have shrunk since the great days of the Romans). He next complains that it is impossible to sleep in a post-chaise (carriage), for you are awakened every half-hour to pay for the next stage, and as there is always an argument about the sum, you cannot perform the transaction while half asleep. At nine o'clock at night he arrives in Paris; it may be the most brilliant capital in the world, but the streets are very dirty. Another short guide-book enumeration of the streets in the various quarters of the city is added here, with more Shandean digressions.

It is a shame that people criticize the French method of travel, says the author, because when you consider the state of the carriages and the poor quality of the horses, it is remarkable that they make any progress at all. The key factor seems to be the bad language they address to the horses, and in particular the two words ***** and ***** (Sterne's asterisks). He dares not write down these words, but he will tell a little story about the abbess of Andouillets to show how she got around the difficulty of using them.

CHAPTERS 21-30

The abbess has tried everything to cure herself of a stiff leg, and finally determines to go to the hot baths of Bourbon.

Comment: The custom of visiting "baths" (usually natural hot springs) in an attempt to cure various ailments by drinking or bathing in the medicinal waters was widespread in Sterne's day. The most famous English spa was at the old Roman baths in the town called Bath, in the west of England.

She takes with her a young novice, and they set off in a carriage drawn by two mules, accompanied by the muleteer. The day is a warm one, and the mule-driver stops off at an inn to refresh himself. The mules, without his prodding, stop in the middle of the road, refusing to go any further. After the two nuns have tried all sorts of things to make them go forward, the younger confesses that she has heard two words that will move any mule, but the words are very sinful. The wise abbess decides that the syllables making up the words are not sinful in themselves, and thus if each of them pronounces one syllable, no sin will be committed. The mules refuse to understand them, "But the devil does," says the abbess.

While the story is being told, the journey has been going on, and Tristram is well on his way south. He now proposes to tell us about an earlier trip taken in company with his father and Uncle Toby. The observations of his elders are so different from those of every other traveler that some of them must be given to the reader. They visit the abbey of St. Germain at Auxerre, and are fascinated by the mummies which a monk shows them; they are both amused and, as good Protestants, a little affronted at his talk of saints and martyrs.

Returning to the more recent expedition, Tristram's chaise breaks down outside of Lyons, and he comforts himself with the idea that he can take a boat down the Rhone to Avignon. He walks about Lyons to see the sights, especially the great cathedral clock and the library of the Jesuits, which contains a famous history of China, written in Chinese. It is hard to account, says the author, for what tourists do; he wants to see these things, although he has absolutely no knowledge of Chinese or the mechanics of clocks.

CHAPTERS 31-43

He sets off to see the tomb of two famous lovers of antiquity, Amandus and Amanda, which is located outside the gates of Lyons, but he is stopped by the sight of a donkey standing in the gate which he must go through. He is moved to reflect on the donkey's sad life, and feels that he is on closer terms with a donkey than with most other animals. His soliloquy is interrupted by an official who says that he must pay for horses for the next post, even though he has determined to go by water; government regulations forbid the traveler to change his mind in the middle of his trip. Tristram receives nothing for the extra six livres he must pay but the knowledge that "fickleness is taxable in France."

Comment: The attitude of most eighteenth-century English travelers toward France was distinctly provincial; they felt that everything was done much better at home. They were most struck by the fact that standards of living were lower, especially for the poor, and that most aspects of life were not as comfortably or as logically organized as in England. Many of the travel-books were largely devoted to complaints, and Sterne, in his Sentimental Journey, makes fun especially of one by the irascible English novelist Tobias Smollett. Our author says that he intends to be much more open-minded and not let little things annoy him, but his account of the episode just described (an almost exact reproduction of one that happened to him) makes it clear that he considers this extra charge one more French imposition on the harmless Englishman, and an additional example of French bureaucracy at work.

At this moment Tristram discovers that he has left his notes of the journey in the broken down chaise, which he has sold to a second-hand dealer. He rushes back and finds that the: lady of the house has used them as curling papers for her hair. She gravely takes them out and returns them; the notes are none the worse, says our hero, for "when they are published ... they will be worse twisted still." He has just time to inspect the tomb of the lovers Amandus and Amanda, but when he gets to the place there is no tomb at all; he wishes Uncle Toby were there to whistle "Lillabullero."

The journey down the river to Avignon is quickly finished, and a mule is hired to travel over the plains of Languedoc. A fertile plain, the author comments, is anathema to most travel writers, for there is nothing for them to describe. Tristam manages things much better, for he describes the people he sees, the little encounters along the road, and in this way is at no loss for anecdotes. He joins the country people at their dances, and wonders why he cannot end his days in this pleasant climate, among such happy people. But there is one obligation left; he has promised to tell the tale of Uncle Toby's amours.

TRISTRAM SHANDY

CHAPTERS 1–10

In the warm and genial climate in which he finds himself, the author protests, it is difficult to keep to the straight line of the story, for he is eternally being distracted. However, his own way of beginning a book seems to him the best of all, and certainly the most devout. He writes the first sentence and trusts to God for the second. As a kind of demonstration of this practice, he begins, "It is with Love as with Cuckoldom - "and breaks off to talk of the fact that words mean different things to different people, to discuss his family, and to wonder why water-drinkers (i.e., men who drink no liquor) are especially attractive to women.

This last remark connects in a tenuous way with the next subject, for Tristram cannot understand why the widow Wadman was so unaccountably attracted to his Uncle Toby. Toby and Corporal Trim have come down from London in such a hurry to begin their military exercises that they have nowhere to stay, and lodge for a few nights with the widow. The author acutely observes that seeing a man living in her own house, among her goods and furniture, makes a woman feel that he should be included in the inventory of her possessions. This connection is apparently made by Mrs. Wadman. Various changes in her behavior, noted by her maid Bridget, make it clear that the widow is in love with Uncle Toby. The Captain's military exercises occupy all his time for eleven years, but at the end of that period he finds leisure for courtship, or, rather, to be courted.

CHAPTERS 11–20

Mrs. Wadman is not content to love in silence, but watches her opportunity. This talk of love makes Tristram reflect on his own difficulties with the opposite sex, and he proceeds to give an alphabet of love, showing that it is: Agitating, Bewitching, Confounded, etc.

The widow's garden adjoins that of Uncle Toby, and a gate makes communication between the two even easier. She becomes extremely interested in the military maneuvers being carried out, and often invades the sentry-box on Toby's bowling green so that he can point out to her the progress of the battle. As the sentry-box is a very small one, hardly large enough for two people, it soon becomes clear that the Captain's fortifications are being attacked in a metaphorical as well as a literal sense; in fact, his defenses are being undermined.

Now that the Peace of Utrecht has made both fortification and siege unnecessary, Uncle Toby and Trim are both downhearted to see the end of their hobby. To console his master. Trim proposes to tell him the story of the King of Bohemia and his seven castles, and begins forthwith. He is, however, constantly interrupted by the Captain's questions, digressions (usually military ones) and remarks on all the subjects under the sun. Mere mention of the King of Bohemia moves Toby to talk about chronology, the importance of geography to the soldier, with examples from the career of his favorite, the Duke of Marlborough, the invention of gunpowder, and any number of other things. The spirit of digression is catching, and presently leads the Corporal and his master into a debate over whether wounds in the knee (like Trim's) or wounds in the groin (like Toby's) are the more painful.

Comment: Trim never does get to tell more than a line or two of his story of the King of Bohemia.

Corporal Trim is reminded of the battle in which he got his wound, and, more important, the fact that he fell head over heels in love with his nurse. The nurse, who takes the Corporal to a peasant's house near the battlefield, is a Beguine, a kind of nun who has not taken permanent vows but devotes her life to good works, such as caring for the sick.

CHAPTERS 21–35

The Corporal manages not to fall in love for a while, but as suddenly and unexpectedly as a shot in the field, he falls. He has hardly ended the story when the widow Wadman, who has been listening all the time, comes through her gate and over to the sentry-box; for her, the opportunity is too good to let slip. She plans to renew her attack on the Captain by asking how the battle is going, but as soon as she realizes that peace has been made, she changes her line and asks Toby to get a piece of sand out of her eye. There is no piece of sand, but the glance of Mrs. Wadman's eye is at least as dangerous as the cannon of Namur, and the Captain falls victim.

The way in which the two brothers react to falling in love demonstrates the difference in their characters. Walter Shandy rebels against the accident, and writes poems against women, while the tender passion only increases Toby's benevolence. The Captain's naivete is such that he sees no reason to keep his love a secret, and tells Trim about it. Captain Toby is all for a declaration of his intentions in proper form, while Trim recommends an immediate assault to carry the lady by storm. The Corporal plans to lay siege to Bridget, the widow's maid, in the kitchen, while his master is confronting Mrs. Wadman in the parlor; both soldiers feel that an attack from two directions at once follows the best military precedents.

Toby's brother teases him about falling in love and proceeds to read him a learned lecture about the various kinds of affection, as described by the ancient authorities on the subject, but Toby shows by his remarks that his own ideas about love are a great deal more sensible and practical than Walter's. Parson Yorick, who is visiting at the time, declares, "I think the procreation of children as beneficial to the world as the finding out the longitude." This attitude seems to agree with the Captain's.

Comment: Navigation was extremely important to England's expanding overseas trade during this period and one of the still unsolved problems was a means for determining longitude. The Admiralty offered a large prize to any mathematician who could devise a method which could be used by ships' captains.

After the group has broken up for the night Tristram's father writes Toby a long letter of instruction, a curious mixture of practical advice based on his own experiences, and lore drawn from his reading of the ancients. Part of the letter deals with recipes for the restraint of lust. On no account must the Captain eat the flesh of goats or deer, but instead should confine himself to a cooling diet, including cucumbers, melons, water lilies and lettuce. Poor Uncle Toby - excessive lust is the least of his problems.

The next morning, just as Uncle Toby and Trim are sallying out to make the attack on the widow, Tristram's father and mother arrive to wish them luck. At this critical juncture. Sterne ends Book VIII.

Comment: Laurence Sterne is in the habit of leaving his readers in suspense, and the present case is no exception. It could be maintained that here he has carried the technique to excess, for his whole audience must have been waiting avidly to find out whether Uncle Toby's court ship met with success. They were forced to wait a year before the next volume appeared.

By this point it seems that Sterne's powers, probably as the result of ill health, were declining. The chapters and the books themselves were becoming shorter and shorter. At the same time he had almost exhausted his material, at least as far as the Shandy family were concerned, and that is one reason he turned farther afield in Books VII and VIII, to Tristram's travels on the Continent and the courtship of the widow Wadman. Yet there are certainly times when the author returns to his earlier skill, and the widow's courtship is among Sterne's most successful blends of sentiment, humor, and mild irony.

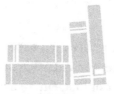

TRISTRAM SHANDY

· ·

CHAPTERS 1-10

The final book of *Tristram Shandy* opens with a "Dedication to A Great Man" which sounds more like the author having a debate with himself. He originally intended to dedicate the volume to Mr. ***, and then bethought himself that Lord **** was a more important figure (the asterisks are Sterne's), though he likes the gentleman just as well as the lord. He hints, too, that he wishes to amuse the audience with a kind of dedication by opposites, for nothing can be more different than the ideas of statesmen (to whom the book is dedicated) and innocent lovers, whose adventures are described within its covers.

Tristram's mother, who with her husband has accompanied Toby to the widow's house, confesses that she would like nothing better than to watch the progress of the affair through the keyhole. Walter humorously takes her to task for her unseemly curiosity, but in this, as he quickly realizes, he is being unfair.

No one, Tristram explains, could possibly have less wantonness or interest in the lascivious than his mother; she is completely phlegmatic by temperament.

> **Comment: Sterne's feelings about his own mother must have been rather ambivalent. She was a rather insensitive and boorish woman who left Laurence to be raised entirely by others, particularly his paternal uncles. When Sterne married an heiress she demonstrated family feeling for the first time; she hurried to England with her daughter so that her son could support her. The sum which Laurence received with his wife was not large, but he offered his mother an annual subsidy. This she refused unless he would guarantee a fund to provide payments if he should die, and further insisted that her pension should come out of the trust before his wife's portion! That, at least, is the way Sterne describes her demands. It was after his refusal of this request that the vicar was accused of letting his mother go to the poorhouse.**

> **These experiences with his mother may have contributed to Sterne's rather odd portrait of Mrs. Shandy. While she is never attacked, only regarded with affectionate amusement, his picture of the acquiescent, almost mindless female is not a very flattering portrait of a woman.**

The Captain and Trim march up to the widow's house in military order. Brave as he is on the field of battle, Toby is terrified of the fair sex, and keeps glancing behind to see that the Corporal is there to support him. His master's nervousness prompts Trim to tell the tale of his brother Tom and the Jew's widow of

Lisbon. The Lisbon widow owns a thriving-sausage shop, and Tom thinks that he can set himself up for life by marrying her. He enters the shop where a kindhearted Negro girl is shooing away the flies, not killing them. At this point Trim breaks off to ask the Captain if Negroes have souls, and is assured that they do, just as surely as white people. The girl, the Corporal adds, was full of natural goodness, and was persecuted only because there was no one to defend her.

> **Comment:** This early example of civil-rights propaganda seems especially topical to us today, and has an interesting background. While Sterne was writing Book IX he received a letter from a Negro named Ignatius Sancho, a servant of the Duke of Montagu. His master gave Sancho the opportunity to educate himself, and he became something of a London celebrity, playing the role of Shakespeare's *Othello* on the stage. The letter begged Sterne to "give half an hour's attention to slavery as it is this day undergone in the West Indies; that subject handled in your own manner, would ease the Yoke of many, perhaps occasion a reformation throughout our Islands ... dear Sir, think in me you behold the uplifted hands of Millions of my moorish brethren." The author was touched by this appeal (which was accompanied by eloquent praise of the earlier volumes of *Tristram Shandy*) and by a "strange coincidence" had just completed the story of the Negro girl.

Trim's brother goes on to speak to the widow who owns the shop. He presents himself frankly as a suitor, and since he is a brisk, good-looking young man, the Jewess accepts him. At this ending to the story, the Captain takes fright again; he seems to fear that his widow may accept him. He does an abrupt about-face and, with Trim, marches away from the widow Wadman's door.

CHAPTERS 11-20

Tristram's father and mother, who have been waiting all this time to see how the encounter will turn out, are surprised and discomfited, and Walter wishes fortification and all the other military arts, cataloged in some detail, at the devil. His wife, as usual, heartily agrees, though she has no idea what he is talking about.

The author remarks that it is necessary to insert a good deal of miscellaneous material at this point if the balance between story and digression, between wisdom and folly, is to be maintained. He turns to each of his virtues and faculties in turn to supply such suitable digressions, but meets with little success. However, he continues, there must be something of genius about him to enable him to write at all, and at least he is open-hearted about it. "... for never do I hit upon any invention or device which tendeth to the furtherance of good writing, but I instantly make it public; willing that all mankind should write as well as myself. - Which they certainly will, when they think as little."

Comment: Here, as in numerous passages throughout the book, Sterne tries to persuade his audience that his writing is entirely spontaneous, the outpourings of a "Shandean" heart. He tries very hard to achieve the effect of spontaneity, but as with most "spontaneous" writing, his effects are usually carefully calculated. For example, he constantly hints at events which are to take place later in the story; the courtship of the widow Wadman is mentioned several books before we get to the encounter itself, and thus our curiosity is whetted. Nearer the beginning of the book, we can also see how the successive accidents, the flattening of Tristram's nose, his christening, and his misadventure in the window, though they seem to be introduced at random, actually work together to confirm Walter Shandy's fears about the future of his son.

His style of writing, the author continues, is also affected by the way he is dressed, and whether he is shaved or not. If he dresses like a gentleman, his writing becomes "genteelized" as well. Female writers, he admits, are at a disadvantage here, for they cannot shave, at least most of them do not need to. Having added the requisite number of digressions, Sterne feels that he can go on with the story.

Toby and Corporal Trim, who are still marching away from the widow's, think better of the matter and return, and Trim knocks at the door. The maid Bridget is waiting with her hand on the latch, and there is little delay in opening. Uncle Toby, seeing that there is no hope for it, begins to whistle "Lillabullero." Tristram draws a curtain over the events of the next few minutes - Chapter 18 is blank, and Chapter 19 is devoted to the words and music of "Lillabullero," while the beginning of Chapter 20 is devoted to a series of asterisks, indicating the beginning of the conversation between Toby and the widow. When we are again allowed to overhear the proceedings, the Captain is offering to show the widow exactly where he received his wound. Toby intends to show her the location on the map, but the widow, blushing, thinks he means something else, and is torn between curiosity and confusion.

CHAPTERS 20-33

There are any number of different reasons why a woman chooses a husband. Tristram returns to his authority on noses, Slawkenbergius, for **imagery** with which to describe this process, but the figures the learned German chooses are very ridiculous ones. He uses the image of donkeys with panniers on their backs - a woman chooses the one which is best loaded. It seems strange that in this world, where Nature has designed everything so well for its purpose, she should have bungled so badly in making the married man. Uncle Toby, on the other hand, has been designed to make an almost perfect husband; he is chivalrous and tender, generous and humane. However, one doubt overshadows all these virtues in the widow's mind. It is about his wound and its possible effects.

> **Comment: What the widow is wondering about, a question which Sterne coyly skirts and dodges around, is whether or not Uncle Toby has been made impotent by his wound. The author contrives to make this speculation into the central joke of these chapters. The imagery and hints he uses are funny enough, if the reader has a taste for bawdy humor, but are also in distinctly bad taste.**

At this point Tristram turns aside again with an invocation to the spirit of humor, and then to tell the story of Maria. Maria is an Italian shepherdess who has gone mad because her wedding bands have been forbidden by a rascally curate. She sits by the side of the road with her pet goat, playing sad airs on her flute, and she is beautiful. The author expends his most sentimental style upon her, though he cannot resist making a joke about himself as well.

We now return to the eighteenth chapter, which has previously been left blank. The Captain marches up to Mrs. Wadman and delivers his declaration of love point-blank. Having made his statement, he has nothing more to say on the subject, and leaves the widow to carry on the conversation by herself. Seeing a Bible on the table, he picks it up and begins to read about the siege of Jericho. The widow is still curious about Toby's wound, but all the satisfaction she receives is a detailed geographical explanation based upon the map of Namur. Trim and Bridget, who are less afflicted with modesty because of their lower station in life, are able to clear the situation up between them.

Mr. Shandy, as one of the large landowners in the parish, keeps a bull to service his own and his neighbors' cows. But the parish is a large one, and the bull is unequal to the demands upon him, and the expected calves do not arrive. With this appropriate but indelicate little allegory on Uncle Toby's situation, *Tristram Shandy* ends. We are never told the final result of the Captain's courtship.

Comment: Although Sterne considered *Tristram Shandy* finished at this point, there is every indication that he could have made good on his promise to produce two volumes a year "forever." But Death, whom he had been fleeing on his travels around the Continent, finally caught up with him. The final volume of his work was published in January, 1767, and he died in March, 1768.

TRISTRAM SHANDY

CHARACTER ANALYSES

A discussion of the characters of *Tristram Shandy* is made more difficult in one respect and easier in another by Sterne's unconventional techniques of writing. Unlike the usual novel, the author is explicitly describing his characters a good deal of the time; we can see the method at work in the recurring sketches of Uncle Toby and the still more frequent and elaborate word-portraits of Walter Shandy. From one point of view, then, we have only to assemble the observations the author himself makes and interject a few comments of our own. The job is further simplified because the personalities of the major characters do not change during the story. Sterne intends them as examples of a specific type, a kind of diagram of a particular "humour," a fixed idea or "ruling passion" at work. The ruling passion is something inherent, and thus always the same. Although Uncle Toby turns his attention from fortifications to courtship at the end of the book, he brings the same frame of mind, the same techniques, even the same vocabulary to his love affair as he brought to the siege of Namur. The author derives a good deal of his humor from this lack of adaptability.

At the same time, we are accustomed to deriving our ideas about character from the interaction of the figures. In more ordinary novels, personalities are illustrated in this way. But in *Tristram Shandy* there is comparatively little of this interaction. Either the characters carry on extended monologues, like Walter Shandy, or they are almost inarticulate, like his wife. Almost the only people between whom real conversations take place are Uncle Toby and Corporal Trim. To read *Tristram Shandy* with appreciation, we must readjust our ideas of what constitutes characterization.

TRISTRAM SHANDY

The confusing time-scheme of the novel makes it important that we specify which Tristram we are talking about. As a figure in the story, he is an infant (or not born yet) for the largest portion of the book, and thus has no character. We do see him as an adult for a short time during his travels in France and Italy, but the clearest impression we derive is of Tristram as the writer, the one who is always directing asides to the reader and commenting upon the action. This side of Tristram Shandy is a persona of Sterne himself, a sort of thin disguise which the real author puts on when he wants to appear before his readers.

Sterne intends his readers to see that the successive accidents which befall the child produce the character of the Tristram whom we see as the writer of the book. The accident to his nose accounts for his inability to stick to one subject and the apparent lack of any fixed purpose in his life. The misfortune of the falling window sash perhaps contributes to his shyness with the fair sex, while the mischance which gives him the wrong name insures that he will never be a leader, but always the onlooker, just as we see him in Tristram Shandy.

The glimpse of Tristram as a young man on his travels (Book VII) provides another side of his personality. We should remember that in his travel-writing, in both the short passage in *Tristram Shandy* and the much longer *Sentimental Journey*, Sterne is attempting to rebut or provide an antidote to the rather bad-tempered guide-books which Englishmen usually wrote. The young traveler tries to be optimistic and amiable, to see the good qualities of foreigners as well as the bad ones. In his travels on the Continent, Tristram is particularly sensible of the pathetic situation, to the misfortunes which fall upon people, especially poor people, through no fault of their own. He also has a sharp eye out for a pretty girl, such as the innkeeper's daughter Janatone. And when the two come together, a pretty girl in misfortune, the result is good for a whole **episode**. Sterne gives us such an **episode** in the pathetic and sentimental story of Maria. In the warmth of the South, Tristram's sensuality comes to the fore. He thinks how he would like to spend the rest of his days in this balmy climate, surrounded by carefree, joyous people.

Tristram as author is whimsical, interested in all sorts of odd bits of knowledge, impulsive and sentimental. In many ways, of course, Tristram is Sterne himself; their likes and dislikes are usually the same. Tristram corresponds to the public image of himself as writer which Sterne tried, quite successfully, to set up. Contemporary readers of *Tristram Shandy* thought of the author as an extraordinarily witty, amusing man, with a deep knowledge of human nature.

WALTER SHANDY

Tristram's father, like his brother Toby, is an example of a man completely devoted to a dominant interest, or "ruling passion." In Walter's case this takes the form of an ungovernable enthusiasm for philosophy and philosophical speculation. He is a classicist, constantly referring to the ancient Greek and Roman authorities for answers to his problems. The more obscure the source, the happier he is with it. Sterne derives a good deal of amusement from the fact that the answers to everyday problems which Mr. Shandy obtains from his ancient authorities are usually quite inadequate ones. In his portrait of Walter Shandy, Sterne is attacking pedantry and useless knowledge in the way that John Locke did. Our author is essentially pragmatic; for him, speculation is purposeless unless it leads to some usable result.

Walter's treatment of his wife is based upon a kind of amused contempt, and in this he follows the classical attitude toward women. He lacks the insight to realize that they fail to communicate with each other, in part, because he assumes in advance that nothing Mrs. Shandy says is worth listening to. Walter's brother Toby is naive but he is aware of the failing; Walter is more naive, because he thinks he is wise.

UNCLE TOBY

If Walter Shandy's ruling passion is philosophy, Uncle Toby's is the military art. For his portrait Sterne makes use of a type from earlier fiction, the gentle soldier. It is the paradoxical contrast between the roughness of his profession and the sweetness of his nature that intrigues readers. He is usually considered the most likable and amiable character in the novel.

In most practical areas of life that do not impinge on his enthusiasm for fortification, Toby is remarkably sensible and level-headed. His brother thinks the Captain ignorant because he cannot follow Walter's wild flights of speculation or his constant references to abstruse books, but in the matter of day-to-day living, Toby is far more successful. As we have pointed out, at least the old soldier is aware of his naivete.

Sterne apparently intends Toby as an example of the "natural man," one uncorrupted by the evils of civilization. The French philosopher Rousseau was helping to make this concept a very popular one at the time. Though Tristram's uncle is impulsive, his impulses are always on the side of goodness. His kindness is particularly evident in the way he treats his servant, Corporal Trim, and in his dealings with the dying soldier Le Fever and his son. The two former comrades-in-arms, the Captain and the Corporal, complement each other's personalities, and together they make up the pleasantest household imaginable.

Toby shows fear only in his dealings with women. As the author tells us, the wound in his groin received at the battle of Namur, the immediate cause for his amateur interest in campaigns and fortifications, is also the reason for his extreme modesty. Sterne is not being entirely candid with us here, for he implies, with a good deal of ribald humor, that the Captain's wound has made him impotent. Yet we have Trim's word during the parley with Bridget at the end of the book that this is not the case.

TRISTRAM'S MOTHER

In spite of her importance as the means of Tristram's appearance on the scene, Mrs. Shandy is a very minor figure in the novel.

Tristram himself says that she has no character at all; she is a caricature of the completely acquiescent wife. Perhaps her habit of agreeing to everything her husband says is sensible enough, for she understands hardly any of his statements. It has already been pointed out that Sterne's portrayal of Mrs. Shandy may be the result of mixed feelings towards his own mother.

CORPORAL TRIM

The Corporal is an example of the simple but good-hearted man, a less educated version of Uncle Toby, and on a lower social level, but possessed of the same real benevolence. In a limited sense, Sterne is democratic; the "lower orders" in his novel have just as many basic virtues as their social betters. Trim is not afraid of action, as his master tends to be, nor does he feel any need to conceal his emotions. His sermon on conscience and the story of Le Fever, as well as the tale of his own brother Tom, all allow us to see Trim's sympathetic nature. At the same time they allow the author to indulge in essays in the pathetic or sentimental mode. Much of the sentimentality of Tristram Shandy is associated with Corporal Trim.

PARSON YORICK

In presenting Parson Yorick, Sterne gives us another aspect of himself. Yorick is the public figure of Sterne as clergyman, while Tristram is Sterne the man. We see Yorick as a "humorous" person, full of little quirks and oddities, but on friendly terms with his neighbors and always ready for a joke or an evening of discussion and entertainment. He is completely orthodox, defending the Established Church against Catholics such as

Dr. Slop. Sterne adopted "Yorick" as his own nickname when he went to London and behaved in the way that Yorick was expected to. The name is derived from that of the dead jester in Shakespeare's *Hamlet*, to whose skull Prince Hamlet addresses one of his soliloquies on mortality. Shakespeare's Yorick is "a fellow of infinite jest," who is wont to "set the tables in a roar," and both Parson Yorick and Sterne do their best to live up to that description.

TRISTRAM SHANDY

CRITICAL ATTITUDES TOWARDS TRISTRAM SHANDY

The works of Laurence Sterne have always disturbed critics, in large part because they are so difficult to categorize. After all, *Tristram Shandy* is not really a novel, nor an essay, nor even a memoir. It is a form compounded of all three, and unique with Sterne. Critics, then, have tended to dismiss the form of the book with phrases like "delightfully haphazard" or "horribly confused" (depending on their attitude toward the writer) and turn their attention to the content. But here they find themselves in almost equal difficulties. How seriously should they take *Tristram Shandy*? Should it be considered inspired fooling all the way through? Does its emphasis on the comic side of life remove it from consideration as serious literature? Or is Sterne really making profound statements in a disguised form, letting us look at our own follies in their nakedness? These are questions on which critics of the author's own time, those of the nineteenth century, and to some degree even those of today, find themselves in basic disagreement.

CONTEMPORARY CRITICS

Sterne's contemporaries appear to have been split in their reception of *Tristram Shandy* between adulation of the author and a rather spiteful criticism which seems to have had a large admixture of professional jealousy. The book was, after all, tremendously successful, and envy was to be expected. Typical of the more rational criticisms were those of the English lexicographer and critic Samuel Johnson. He objected to the disorderly nature of the work, and to Sterne's obscenity and irreligious comments, which Johnson felt were unsuitable for a clergyman. Admirers of the book, including the famous actor David Garrick, liked its wit, its deflation of conventional values, and the sentimental **episodes** which Sterne introduced. Even his friends were not disposed to give Sterne much credit for deep thinking. For most contemporary readers, it hit exactly the right balance between the humorous and the pathetic. Even the famous German writer Goethe is supposed to have said of *Tristram Shandy*, "... it is not every kind of humor that leaves the soul calm and serene."

LATER CRITICS

Nineteenth-century critics, especially those of the Victorian era, were generally loud in their denunciation of Sterne's immorality and obscenity, and were content to miss most of his humor completely. In our own day, in keeping with the modern trend toward close analysis, there has been an emphasis on Sterne's serious side, an attempt to see a deeper meaning in his surface fooling. In their effort to explain the pattern of *Tristram Shandy*, and thus to make the structure of the book clearer, these criticisms are very helpful. The reader of such explanatory essays should remember, however, that serious critics are looking for the serious in any work they examine. Humor is, by its nature, not very susceptible to critical analysis; even when it is analyzed successfully it is no longer humor. Modern scholars are inclined to accept as already understood the fact that *Tristram Shandy* is a very funny book.

A PHILOSOPHICAL FRAMEWORK

One of the best of the attempts to establish a philosophical basis for Sterne's work is found in John Traugott's *Tristram Shandy's World*. Traugott's explanation relies heavily on two points: Sterne's interest in the works of the English philosopher John Locke, especially the *Essay Concerning Human Understanding* (Sterne refers to Locke constantly throughout his book), and our author's innate skepticism. According to Traugott, the author of *Tristram Shandy* admired Locke's attempt to provide a rational explanation and analysis of human thought and communication, but he also wished to point out that any exclusively rational explanation of man's conduct is necessarily incomplete. Some of our most basic acts are irrational. Sterne argues for a recognition of the importance of sentiment or whim or impulse in our thinking, even when we think we are being most logical. He feels that wit can be as powerful a tool in understanding the nature of communication as logic. As an example, Traugott points out that Walter Shandy and his brother Toby hardly communicate at all on a rational level, yet they do communicate, because of their sympathy with each other.

LOCKE AND THE PROBLEM OF COMMUNICATION

A basic tenet of Locke's study of communication is that a human being is a single, unchanging person. Yet, Sterne points out, each of us is not a single person but many people; we present a different mask to each person we know, and this is not a matter of deceit, but an unconscious adaptation - part of our personality. To paraphrase Traugott's perceptive remark, evil, for Sterne, is thinking that you alone do not wear a mask. Locke and Sterne were alike in their hatred of intellectual poseurs and learned fakery, and their works are, in wholly different ways, attacks on these abuses of reason. But paradoxically (and Laurence Sterne was fully aware of the paradoxes in human nature, his own included) our author attacks Locke because he admires him. The Slawkenbergius **epic**, for instance, satirizes rationalism from start to finish; here reason creates confusion instead of dispelling it, and divides people instead of bringing them together.

SOURCES FOR TRISTRAM SHANDY

A number of critics have devoted themselves to a study of the sources of Sterne's material and to finding the origin of the Shandean style. Sources are discussed in detail in Wilbur L. Cross's comprehensive biography, *The Life and Times of Laurence Sterne*. Cross says that *Tristram Shandy* is indebted for specific ideas and to some extent for style to Sterne's avowed models; the sixteenth-century French satirist Francois Rabelais with his *Gargantua and Pantagruel*, Miguel Cervantes' *Don Quixote*, the famous sixteenth-century Spanish novel of the humorous and pathetic, and John Locke's philosophical writings. He maintains, however, that the influences our author does not acknowledge are even more important, especially Robert Burton's essay, "The Anatomy of Melancholy", written in the seventeenth century, from which Sterne could have borrowed much of his discursive technique and apparently whimsical choice of subject matter. A predecessor even closer in time is Jonathan Swift, whose *Tale of a Tub* (1704) is extremely similar to Sterne's early **satire**, *The History of a Good Warm Watchcoat*.

Also interested in Sterne's sources is Margaret Shaw in her *Laurence Sterne: the Making of a Humorist*, who points out the novelist's debt to the French essayist Montaigne. Miss Shaw also speculates in an interesting way on just what made Sterne the kind of man he was, and looks to his family background and the pressures of his time for an explanation of his personality. J. A. Work's edition of *Tristram Shandy* is the most complete one available, with very thorough explanatory notes. Work's introduction is also one of the best general appraisals of the novel, discussing in a balanced way the characters, the form of the work, and the reasons for Sterne's peculiarities of style.

STERNE'S SENTIMENTALITY

In *The Unsentimental Journey of Laurence Sterne*, Ernest N. Dilworth discusses the matter of sentiment. He concludes that Sterne meant the sentimental passages to be taken humorously; we are supposed to laugh at Maria, or at least at the picture of Maria and Tristram together, not weep for her. Dilworth maintains that Sterne is too thorough a jester for most people's taste; he makes fun of everything, including the reader's most deeply felt emotions. In this he agrees with John Traugott. Both feel that our author deliberately tries to make the audience emotionally involved with a character or situation, and then, by a twist in the story, makes us laugh both at the character, and at ourselves for being taken in.

THE PROBLEM OF FORM

The problem of the form of *Tristram Shandy*, or rather the lack of it, is one that has baffled a good many critics. One solution is provided by B. H. Lehman in his article "Of Time, Personality and the Author: A Study of *Tristram Shandy's* Comedy." Lehman argues that Sterne felt constricted by the rigid form adopted by earlier novelists. With his comprehensive and pragmatic view of life, he considered that their works made things seem too orderly and intelligible to be true. In his rebellion in favor of a much more discursive, less rigid form, he is the predecessor of many important novelists much closer to our own time-writers such as James Joyce and his *Ulysses*, Marcel Proust with his *Remembrance of Things Past*, and Thomas Mann's *Magic Mountain*. Certainly Sterne is experimenting with the relativity of time, as they are, and like them is involved with word-play and the association of ideas.

STERNE'S ACHIEVEMENT

The modern tendency, then, is to see Sterne not only as the jester but as the serious thinker as well. He is concerned with human relationships and the difficulty of communication between people, though he is aware that communication can take many forms other than speech. Attempts to provide an ethical and philosophical framework for *Tristram Shandy* are suggestive but not wholly convincing. While it is interesting and helpful to know that Sterne is preoccupied with Locke's ideas and skeptical of Locke's emphasis on reason, it would be going too far to say that the author intended to write his novel solely as a declaration of his own ideas. On a far more mundane level, Laurence Sterne set out to be a famous author, and chose a topic and a style which he thought would help him attain this goal. That he chose well, the immense vogue of *Tristram Shandy* in his own day and its continuing popularity in ours provide ample evidence.

TRISTRAM SHANDY

ESSAY QUESTIONS AND ANSWERS

. . . .

Question: What are some of the effects which Sterne achieves by means of the "Shandean" style?

Answer: The average reader is first confused by the peculiarities of Sterne's style, then amused by it, and finally intrigued by the possibility that it may have some relation with what, in the larger sense, the author is trying to say. The author certainly does intend us to be amused at his multitude of digressions, his habit of jumping from one subject to another, but the style of *Tristram Shandy* also provides us with a hint of Sterne's own view of life.

Laurence Sterne's style is one of his chief sources of humor, and the amusement lies largely in the fact that he is continually defeating our expectations and confronting us with the unexpected. He tells us a sentimental story, and just when we expect to be reduced to tears by the ending, he figuratively thumbs his nose at us and makes us laugh. Yet this continual reversal of what we look forward to can also give us an insight into Sterne's more serious attitudes.

He tells us, repeatedly, with a perfectly straight face, that there is nothing fantastic about his tale. It is simply a view of what life is like. If for once he is telling us the truth, then life, for Sterne, does not continue in straight lines to a logical ending, but insists on going off in all sorts of directions, despite our attempts to control it. The more we think about this proposition, at least under Sterne's influence, the more we realize that it is true. In the same way, the characters of *Tristram Shandy* seem unable to keep their thoughts under any sort of control. One thought continually brings up another which is related to it only by some indirect association, and this in turn starts a whole new train of ideas. Gradually we realize that we think in the same way. By means of his style Sterne can make fun of the conventional ideas of cause and effect, and of logic itself. He is constantly whispering to us, "You think your life is so logical, but is it really? Of course not!"

At the same time, the author makes fun of our ideas of time. As he points out, it may have taken him several days to write a chapter; that is his time. We the readers may read it in half an hour; that is our time. But the chapter itself may describe the thoughts which are going through a character's mind in an instant. That is the character's time. Now all these different intervals deal with the same set of events. Which is the "true" amount of time which has elapsed - the time of the writer, the reader, or the character? Sterne loves to set us such unanswerable conundrums, to prove that seemingly "logical" questions do not have equally logical answers.

Of course, the Shandean style is also useful in a purely mechanical way. He can use it to put off the **climax** of a story indefinitely, and thus raise our suspense. It can also be utilized to prolong the book indefinitely, until it seems as if Sterne is making good on his promise to keep on writing "forever."

The Shandean style, then, is an integral part of Sterne's work. It reflects the nature of the man, as any good style must, and it enables him to amuse us and to put forward his own ideas in an unusually effective way.

Question: How does Sterne make clear the family relationship between Tristram, his father, and Uncle Toby?

Answer: In portraying these three characters (and many others) Sterne had in mind the theory of the humors, the idea that most men are controlled by a "ruling passion." This ruling passion is determined in part by the stars under which we are born, and more directly by our physical makeup, which is related to heredity. According to eighteenth-century ideas of heredity, it would be logical to expect all three men of the Shandy family to pursue a single interest or idea to excess, though the direction these interests took might be completely different. All three are variations on the same basic character. In the case of Walter Shandy, his ruling passion is the love of philosophy, of speculation and theorizing. He respects theory so much, particularly the theories of the ancients, that he tries to apply them to the problems of everyday life whether they are realty appropriate or not, and the results are disastrous.

Uncle Toby, though he is sensible enough in other directions, has an attraction to the military arts, particularly to fortification, approaching madness. He tries to interpret everything he sees or hears in military terms, to the annoyance of his brother.

Tristram's guiding impulse is a little harder to pin down, but as we read the book it becomes clear. Young Tristram, after all, is the one who is telling the story, and his passion is the one that rules the novel - unreason or illogic. He follows this principle as faithfully as his father follows reason. Sterne had a clear insight into human nature; he makes Tristram's ruling passion the opposite of his father's.

As a final characteristic linking the main figures of the novel, we should notice that all three have the same basic amiability, or love of mankind. Walter's expression of this state of mind is somewhat masked by his apparent peevishness, what Sterne calls his "subacid drollery," but his essentially good heart shines through. For example, he does not fly into a rage at the successive **catastrophes** to his son, Tristram, but accepts them resignedly. He calls this philosophy, but it is really good humor. If the Shandys, father and son and uncle, are divided by their passions, they are also united by their benevolence.

Question: In what ways does *Tristram Shandy* look forward to the modern novel?

Answer: With regard to some aspects of novel-writing, Sterne seems far ahead of his time. He appears to be dissatisfied with the traditional structure of the novel during his era, which attempted to divide life into neat segments of time and to follow a logical plot. If the aim of the novel is **realism**, our author is well aware that life is neither as simple nor as neatly segmented as his contemporaries seem to think. A truly realistic novel would have to take in all the vagaries of human behavior, all the illogic and the apparently pointless digressions of which our lives are really made up.

In *Tristram Shandy*, then, Sterne is creating a new kind of **realism**, even though his primary purpose for doing so may have been the comic effect. He knew, as most of his fellow writers did not, that people's ideas are as important (and as interesting to the audience) as their actions. The digressions of the book contribute to our picture of the characters, particularly to that of Tristram himself, even though they do not advance the action. A good many modern novelists use the same kind of indirect characterization today.

Sterne's characterization may also be seen as comparatively realistic. The characters of even a good eighteenth-century novelist, such as Henry Fielding, are stereotypes when contrasted with Tristram or Uncle Toby. When we find out that Fielding's Squire Allworthy, in Tom Jones, is the benevolent country squire, we know practically all that there is to learn about him. The figures of *Tristram Shandy*, on the other hand, are continually presenting us with unexpected aspects of themselves, even if they are not completely three-dimensional.

A number of other features which we have come to think of as modern can be found in Sterne's novel. He plays with the idea of time, showing his awareness of the fact that time is relative, not absolute. The sense of duration may be different for each person. He makes fun of our ideas of logic and demonstrates that human relationships are carried on by illogical means, not logical ones. Scenes and ideas are connected by association rather than chronology. To generalize, Laurence Sterne shows a striking awareness of the way the human mind works. All his literary tricks, his quirks and jokes upon the reader, in fact the whole structure of his book, are based upon the knowledge of human nature. Perhaps Sterne is most modern because he attempts, to the best of his ability, to show us as we know we are, rather than as we assume other people to be. When we consider others we tend to think in stereotypes, though we know the generalizations are not true of ourselves. Sterne reminds us that the generalizations are not true of others, either.

GLOSSARY OF TERMS

. . . .

Beguine: A woman belonging to a religious order who does not take vows but does good works, attending the sick, etc.

Catachresis: A rhetorical error, misuse or abuse of terms.

Cataplasm: A poultice or dressing for a wound.

Chaise-Vamper: A dealer in and repairer of chaises (small horse-drawn carriages).

Civilian: A lawyer. An expert in civil law (as opposed to an expert in canon, or church law, who is called a canonist).

Crasis: Temperament or natural constitution - personality.

Facete: Witty, amusing.

Fardel: A burden or bundle.

Granado: A hand grenade.

Hussive: A small case for needles, pins, thread, etc. The word is a derivative of "housewife."

BRIGHT NOTES STUDY GUIDE

Hypallage: A rhetorical term meaning the inversion of two words or ideas so that they are no longer in their natural order.

Jointure, Marriage Settlement: A sum of money or piece of income producing property assigned to the wife at marriage, usually in return for the dowry which her parents give the husband.

Pantofles: Slippers.

Puisne: Small, inferior. We now spell the word puny.

Sack: Sherry wine.

Tabid: Progressively emaciated, wasted away.

Tackling: The rigging of a ship, especially a sailing ship.

Term-Time: The period of time when court is in session.

Thrum: The end of a piece of yarn.

Tritical: Trite, worn out by use.

Trope: Rhetorical term - a figure of speech.

Videnda: Things which ought to be seen.

BIBLIOGRAPHY

The following list contains recent biographies of Sterne and critical works on *Tristram Shandy*. Biographies written before 1900 have been superseded by more recent ones because of new material discovered in this century, and because material once suppressed has finally been published. In the same way, modern editions of Sterne's letters are reliable, but older ones mutilated or expurgated his correspondence.

Connely, Willard. *Laurence Sterne as Yorick*. London: The Bodley Head Press, 1958. This very capable and detailed life of Sterne concentrates on his literary career, and also provides interesting details of the eighteenth-century literary scene.

Cross, Wilbur L. *The Life and Times of Laurence Sterne*. Third edition. New Haven: Yale University Press, 1929. Cross has produced the definitive biography of Sterne and included much critical information as well. He also provides many details of the lives of Sterne's friends and relatives.

Curtis, Lewis P. *The Politicks of Laurence Sterne*. London: Oxford University Press, 1929. Curtis' book concentrates on Sterne's articles for local periodicals, *the York Journal* and *The Protestant Courant*. The author's political career, however, throws much light on the attitudes and prejudices of *Tristram Shandy*.

Dilworth, Ernest N. *The Unsentimental Journey of Laurence Sterne*. New York: King's Crown Press, 1948. In this discussion of Sterne's use of the sentimental, Dilworth concludes that sentimental scenes are included for humorous effect, to make us laugh at our own susceptibility.

Fredman, Alice G. *Diderot and Sterne*. New York: Columbia University Press, 1955. Dr. Fredman shows the close relationship between the English humorist and his French counterpart, and demonstrates their importance in the changes of attitude and taste which led to Romanticism.

Jefferson, D. W. "*Tristram Shandy* and the Tradition of Learned Wit," *Essays in Criticism*, I, (1951), pp. 225–248. Jefferson's important article provides a basis for understanding both content and form of the novel as part of the tradition of learned wit, in the line of Rabelais and Swift.

Lehman, B. H. "Of Time, Personality and the Author: A Study of Tristram Shandy's Comedy," in *Studies in the Comic*, University of California Publications in English, VIII, No. 2 (1941), pp. 233–250. A contribution to the view of *Tristram Shandy* as a serious philosophic work, Lehman's article also points out how many of Sterne's devices are used by later important novelists.

Shaw, Margaret R. B. *Laurence Sterne: the Making of a Humorist*. London: The Richards Press, 1957. A readable biography with some criticism of *Tristram Shandy*, Miss Shaw's book attempts to find the sources of Sterne's genius in his family background and wide reading.

Sterne, Laurence. *The Letters of Laurence Sterne*. Edited by Lewis Perry Curtis. Oxford: Clarendon Press, 1935. Sterne's letters are, of course, indispensable for a complete understanding of his work. It is remarkable to see how he adapts the characters of Tristram and Parson Yorick, even in letters to personal friends.

_____. *The Life and Opinions of Tristram Shandy, Gentleman.* Introduction by Bergen Evans. Modern Library Edition. New York: Random House, 1950. This is the most widely available edition of *Tristram Shandy.* The Introduction by Bergen Evans is helpful on general points, but the book lacks explanatory notes.

_____. *The Life and Opinions of Tristram Shandy, Gentleman.* Edited by James A. Work. New York: The Odyssey Press, 1940. The Introduction provided by Work, together with complete explanatory notes, translations of all passages in foreign languages, etc., make this by far the most useful edition of *Tristram Shandy.*

Traugott, John. *Tristram Shandy's World: Sterne's Philosophical Rhetoric.* Berkeley, Cal.: University of California Press, 1954. Traugott's book is one of the best modern attempts to provide a philosophical framework for *Tristram Shandy.* He bases his ideas on Sterne's attitude, both admiring and critical, toward Locke's rationalism, and on their common hatred for learned pretension and pedantry.

Watkins, W. B. C. *Perilous Balance: The Tragic Genius of Swift, Johnson, and Sterne.* Cambridge: Walker-de Berry, Inc., 1960. An intriguing attempt at a psychological portrait within a small compass, Watkins' book tries to see the effect on Sterne's work of his personality and his illness.

EXPLORE THE ENTIRE LIBRARY OF BRIGHT NOTES STUDY GUIDES

From Shakespeare to Sinclair Lewis and from Plato to Pearl S. Buck, The Bright Notes Study Guide library spans hundreds of volumes, providing clear and comprehensive insights into the world's greatest literature. Discover more, faster with the Bright Notes Study Guide to the classics you're reading today.

See the entire library of available
Bright Notes guides at **BrightNotes.com**

Available in print and digital wherever books are sold

IP INFLUENCE PUBLISHERS

CPSIA information can be obtained
at www.ICGtesting.com
Printed in the USA
BVHW091930300421
606221BV00013B/2055

9 781645 424086